Preparing for the SHRM-SCP® Exam

Workbook and 70 Practice Questions from SHRM

Second Edition

PREPARING FOR THE SHRM-SCP® EXAM

WORKBOOK AND 70 PRACTICE QUESTIONS FROM SHRM

SECOND EDITION

Editors: Charles Glover, MS Manager, Exam Development & Accreditation, SHRM and Nancy A. Woolever, MAIS, SHRM-SCP, Vice President, Academic, Certification, and Student Communities

SHRM is a member-driven catalyst for creating better workplaces where people and businesses thrive together. As the trusted authority on all things work, SHRM is the foremost expert, researcher, advocate, and thought leader on issues and innovations impacting today's evolving workplaces. With nearly 340,000 members in 180 countries, SHRM touches the lives of more than 362 million workers and their families globally. Discover more at SHRM.org.

ISBN 9781586447328 (paperback)
ISBN 9781586447335 (pdf)
ISBN 9781586447342 (epub)
ISBN 9781586447359 (kindle)

Published in the United States of America

SECOND EDITION   2025 REVISED PRINTING

PB Printing   10 9 8 7 6 5 4 3 2

Contents

Acknowledgments vii

Introduction ix

SECTION 1
THE SHRM-SCP EXAM STRUCTURE

Types of Exam Items. 1

Exam Items 2

Exam Timing. 2

SECTION 2
THE SHRM BASK

Structure of the SHRM BASK 4

How to Use the SHRM BASK for Studying. 8

SECTION 3
USING THE SHRM BASK TO PREPARE FOR THE SHRM-SCP EXAM

HR Expertise Example: Structure of the HR Function 13

Behavioral Competency Example: Relationship
Management 18

Let's Practice! Twenty SHRM-SCP Practice Items and
Answers. 23

SECTION 4
THE SHRM-SCP EXAM BLUEPRINT

Self-Assessment for Your Exam Study Plan. 36

Create a SMART Study Plan 40

Get Started on Your Study Schedule 41

SECTION 5
THE SHRM-SCP FIFTY-ITEM PRACTICE TEST

Introduction. 43

SHRM-SCP Practice Test Questions 44

APPENDIX 1

The SHRM-SCP Practice Test Answers 61

APPENDIX 2

Twelve-Week Study Schedule Template 69

About SHRM Books 83
Index 85

Acknowledgments

This workbook was made possible by the thoughtful and generous advice, guidance, and input of many smart and talented subject matter experts, especially the following:

Mike Aitken, Executive vice president, HR Professional Solutions, SHRM

Alexander Alonso, PhD, SHRM-SCP, chief data & insights officer, SHRM

Nicholas Schacht, SHRM-SCP, chief commercial officer, SHRM

Jeanne Morris, senior vice president, Consumer Products, SHRM

Patricia Byrd, SHRM-SCP, director, Credentialing Services, SHRM

Susie Davis, director, Education Products, SHRM

Hanna Evans, SHRM-CP senior specialist, Form Development, SHRM

Eddice L. Douglas, SHRM-CP, lead, Educational Products, SHRM

Sarah Chuon, SHRM-CP, specialist, Exam Development, SHRM

Giselle Calliste, SHRM-CP, specialist, Exam HR Content, SHRM

Morgan Fecto, Exam Development, SHRM

Scott Oppler, PhD, senior technical advisor, Human Resource Research Organization (HumRRO)

Laura Steighner, PhD, president, Steighner Solutions

Kelly Cusick, senior vice president, Marketing, Holmes Corporation

Caitlin Shea, SHRM-CP, product manager, Holmes Corporation

We also gratefully acknowledge the scores of SHRM members, SHRM certificate holders, and exam candidates who provided input for this book.

Introduction

We applaud your decision to move your career in Human Resources forward by pursuing a certification with SHRM! To this end, this workbook is designed to help you prepare for the **SHRM Senior Certified Professional (SHRM-SCP®)** exam.

Specifically, the SHRM Senior Certified Professional (SHRM-SCP) designation is for HR professionals who are relatively advanced in their careers. This level of professional primarily works in a strategic role, such as developing policies and strategies, overseeing the execution of integrated HR operations, directing the entire HR enterprise, and leading the alignment of HR strategies to organizational goal, and much more. The SHRM-SCP exam is designed to test this *strategic*-level HR knowledge and proficiency.

In this second edition, we have placed a greater emphasis on utilizing and understanding the SHRM Body of Applied Skills and Knowledge (SHRM BASK®)—bridging the knowledge, concepts, and competencies that the SHRM BASK encapsulates to the SHRM-SCP exams. Perhaps most importantly, this workbook includes a total of 70 practice items that were used on past SHRM-SCP exams. These practice items will provide you with more exposure to the types of items that you will see on the real exam, as well as feedback about correct responses. These items were not simply created for this book—they were taken from actual SHRM-SCP exams that were used in previous years.

On the other hand, the SHRM-CP exam is designed to determine who has the level of competency and knowledge that is expected for HR professionals who perform (or will perform) operational work. This includes such duties as implementing policies, serving as the HR point of contact, and performing day-to-day HR functions. Although the SHRM-CP and SHRM-SCP exams are very similar in structure, this workbook is focused exclusively on the SHRM-SCP exam.

It is important to note that this workbook is designed to be used along with the official SHRM study guide: *Ace Your SHRM Certification Exam: The Official SHRM Study Guide for the SHRM-CP and SHRM-SCP Exams*, the SHRM BASK, and the SHRM Learning System®. The study guide includes much additional information about the exam and exam preparation strategies, and it also includes a set of practice items from a combination of the SHRM-CP and SHRM-SCP exams. The SHRM BASK reflects the blueprint for the SHRM-SCP exam and should be used to develop your study plan. The SHRM Learning System is the comprehensive preparation tool offered by SHRM built upon the SHRM BASK.

In this SHRM-SCP workbook, some of the key concepts that were introduced in the study guide are further explained. For example, a self-assessment for gauging strengths and development areas that are addressed in the exam was briefly introduced in the study guide; this is created in the current workbook to help with SHRM-SCP exam preparation.

Thank you for allowing SHRM to embark on this journey with you toward SHRM-SCP certification and beyond!

How to Apply

SHRM offers both certification exams during two testing windows every year. The first window is from May 1 to July 15, and the second window is from December 1 to February 15. Examinees can choose to take the exam in person at one of more than 500 Prometric testing centers across more than 180 countries, or you can choose to take it via live remote proctoring.

Once you have decided which exam to take, register to take the exam on the SHRM website any-time between the Applications Accepted Starting Date and the Standard Application Deadline.

Examinees who apply by the **Early-Bird Application Deadline** and/or who are **SHRM members** receive a reduced exam fee. Note that exam applications apply to specific testing windows; once you have applied, transferring to the next testing window is possible for an additional fee.

To learn more about the benefits of SHRM memberships, receive discounts on the SHRM Learning System and the SHRM Certification exams, and much more, navigate to this link: https://www.shrm.org/membership.

To apply, you must

1. Apply online (https://www.shrm.org/credentials/certification),

2. Create a user account,

3. Select the exam level you want to take,

4. Complete the application form and sign the SHRM Certification Candidate Agreement,

5. Pay the application fee, and

6. Once you receive your Authorization-to-Test (ATT) letter, schedule your exam directly through SHRM's test delivery vendor (https://www.prometric.com/shrm). Your ATT letter will outline several ways to schedule your exam and select your testing location/modality (test in person or via remote proctoring).

SHRM-CP and SHRM-SCP Eligibility

SHRM Certified Professional (SHRM-CP)

- The SHRM-CP certification is intended for individuals who perform general HR or HR-related duties, or for currently enrolled students and individuals pursuing a career in Human Resource Management.
- Candidates for the SHRM-CP certification are not required to hold an HR title and do not need a degree or previous HR experience to apply; however, a basic working knowledge of HR practices and principles or a degree from an Academically Aligned program is recommended.
- The SHRM-CP exam is designed to assess the competency level of HR at the operational level. This level includes implementing policies, supporting day-to-day HR functions, or serving as an HR point of contact for staff and stakeholders.
- Refer to the SHRM BASK for detailed information on proficiency standards for this credential (i.e., Proficiency Indicators only for All HR Professionals).

SHRM Senior Certified Professional (SHRM-SCP)

- The SHRM-SCP certification is for individuals who have a work history of at least **three years performing strategic level HR or HR-related duties,** or for SHRM-CP credential holders who have held the credential for at least three years and are working in, or are in the process of transitioning to, a strategic level role.
- Candidates for the SHRM-SCP certification are not required to hold an HR title and do not need a degree to apply.
- The SHRM-SCP exam is designed to assess the competency level of those who engage in HR work at the strategic level. Work at this level includes duties such as developing HR policies and/or procedures, overseeing the execution of integrated HR operations, directing an entire HR enterprise, or leading the alignment of HR strategies to organizational goals.
- Applicants must be able to demonstrate that they devoted at least 1,000 hours per calendar year (Jan.–Dec.) to strategic-level HR or HR-related work.
  - More than 1,000 hours in a calendar year does not equate to more than one year of experience.
  - Part-time work qualifies as long as the 1,000-hour per calendar year standard is met.
  - Experience may be either salaried or hourly.
- Individuals who are HR consultants may demonstrate qualifying experience through the HR or HR-related duties they perform for their clients. Contracted hours must meet the 1,000-hour standard.
- Refer to the SHRM BASK for detailed information on proficiency standards for this credential (i.e., Proficiency Indicators for All HR Professionals and for Advanced HR Professionals).

🌐 **ONLINE**
Learn More about How to Apply for the Exam

https://www.shrm.org/credentials/certification/how-to-get-shrm-certified-process

Testing Options

Why Might Remote-Proctored Testing Be a Good Option for Me?

There are many reasons people choose to test remotely. One of these reasons might fit your circumstances:

» Testing in a familiar place helps put you at ease.

» The nearest test center is farther away than you wish to travel.

» The convenience of testing anytime and anywhere gives you more control over your experience.

» There are no in-person seats available at the time you want to test.

Why Might Remote-Proctored Testing NOT Be a Good Option for Me?

Remote-proctored testing isn't for everyone. When you take a SHRM certification exam via remote proctoring, your home or office *becomes* the testing center. This means you are responsible for ensuring the security of your exam as well as providing the computer and internet connection to complete the exam. Here are some strong reasons why remote proctoring might *not* be the best option for you:

» You do not have access to a computer that meets Prometric's system requirements.

» You do not have a strong, stable internet connection.

» You do not have a quiet, private room (with a door that closes) at your home or office to take the exam.

» You want to have immediate access to an in-person test center administrator in case something goes wrong with your exam.

To ensure you are making an informed decision, check out this link to decide if remote proctoring or in-person testing is right for you: https://www.prometric.com/proproctorcandidate.

Section 1

The SHRM-SCP Exam Structure

Types of Exam Items

As defined in the *Ace Your SHRM Certification Exam* study guide, and on the SHRM website, there are two general types of items on the SHRM-SCP exam: (1) knowledge items (KIs) and foundational knowledge items (FKIs); and (2) situational judgment items (SJIs).

Knowledge items (including FKIs) are stand-alone multiple-choice items with four response options. Each KI tests a single piece of knowledge or application of knowledge.

Situational judgment items (SJIs) present realistic situations from workplaces throughout the world. Based on the scenario presented, SJIs ask test takers to consider the problem presented in the question within the context of the situation, and then select the best course of action to take. As with the KIs, these are multiple-choice items with four response options.

The distribution of items with respect to content and item type is essentially the same for both the SHRM-SCP and SHRM-CP exams. About half of the items on each exam are allocated across the three behavioral competency clusters, and the other half are allocated across the three HR knowledge domains. Approximately 40% of the items on each exam are situational judgment items, and the remainder are stand-alone items measuring either knowledge that is foundational to the behavioral competencies (10%) or HR-specific knowledge (50%).

Item Type

Situational Judgment (40%)   HR-Specific Knowledge (50%)
Foundational Knowledge (10%)

Behavioral Competency Clusters

Leadership (17%)
Business (16.5%)
Interpersonal (16.5%)

HR Knowledge Domains

People (18%)
Organization (18%)
Workplace (14%)

1

Exam Items

The SHRM-SCP exam consists of a total of 134 questions—110 of the questions are scored, and 24 of the questions are unscored. The purpose of unscored items is to gather data to determine if they are viable to become scored test items on future SHRM exams if they perform well. Think of unscored items like beta testing to gather tester data. While unscored items will not affect your overall score (getting unscored items incorrect will not count against you), it is important not to skip any questions.

The scored and unscored items are intermingled throughout the exam and are indiscernible from one another. This exam is broken into two equal halves, and each half contains 67 questions.

Each half is divided into three sections:

» **Section 1**: 20 KIs and FKIs (i.e., knowledge items for behavioral competencies)

» **Section 2**: 27 SJIs

» **Section 3**: 20 KIs and FKIs

Exam Timing

The total exam appointment time is four hours, which includes **three hours and forty minutes** of testing time for the exam itself. This equals approximately 90 seconds per question. It is important to use your time wisely.

It is critical to note that you will be unable to return to Exam Half 1 upon moving to Exam Half 2. Ensure that you have answered all of the questions to the best of your ability in Exam Half 1 before proceeding to the second half of the exam. There will be confirmatory prompts for you before transitioning to Exam Half 2.

The exam time is broken down into the following segments:

» **Introduction**, including confidentiality reminder: four minutes

» **Tutorial**: eight minutes

» **Exam Half 1**: up to one hour and fifty minutes

» **Exam Half 2**: up to one hour and fifty minutes

» **Post Exam Survey**: six minutes

There are a few transition screens throughout the exam that account for the remaining minutes.

Section 2

The SHRM BASK

One of the most important things for you to understand as you prepare for the SHRM-SCP exam is this:

All of the HR competencies and knowledge areas that are assessed on the SHRM-SCP exam are detailed in the SHRM BASK.

Conceptually, preparing for the SHRM-SCP exam is not unlike preparing for the SHRM-CP exam. Do not be fooled, however, they are completely different exams by design, emphasizing differences found in the **proficiency indicators** area of the SHRM BASK. You may be tempted to rely on your professional experience as preparation. Alternatively, if you have taken the SHRM-CP, rely on your preparation and knowledge gained to carry you through the SHRM-SCP exam. It is critical to match your knowledge and experience with the key concepts and proficiency indicators with those in the SHRM BASK for **Advanced HR Professionals** ensuring you feel comfortable and confident with the material. If not, the SHRM-CP may be the best place to begin your journey until you are ready to elevate your credentials.

While the SHRM-CP and SHRM-SCP share the same blueprint, the exams are designed to be completely distinct by way of using proficiency indicators to separate the knowledge, skills, and abilities required to address *operational-level* (SHRM-CP) HR duties and tasks versus *strategic-level* (SHRM-SCP) HR functions and responsibilities.

The SHRM BASK can also be thought of as the blueprint for the SHRM-SCP exam, much like an architect uses a blueprint to construct a building, testing programs use an 'exam blueprint' to build examinations. You can find the complete version of the SHRM BASK at:

https://www.shrm.org/credentials/certification/exam-preparation/
body-of-applied-skills-and-knowledge

Important reminders as you prepare for the SHRM-SCP exam:

» If something is not covered in the SHRM BASK, it is not eligible for the SHRM-SCP exam. However, the SHRM BASK is an expansive document that covers many different areas, and given its breadth, you might not see everything that is presented in the SHRM BASK represented on the SHRM-SCP exam in any given testing window.

» The SHRM BASK does not define your specific HR role, but rather the HR professional role in general. Therefore, it may cover more than your current or past HR roles.

» For individuals testing outside of the U.S., you are not held accountable for content covered in the U.S. Employment Law & Regulations section of the SHRM BASK (Workplace content domain). Those items will be substituted with items from the Workplace domain.

Figure 2.1. The SHRM BASK Model

This workbook is designed to demystify the SHRM BASK, providing insights to aid your test preparation using the SHRM BASK as a study tool. In this section, we provide guidance on how to break the SHRM BASK into digestible segments to help you identify areas of strength and areas that you need to study more, ultimately creating a personalized study guide in preparation for the SHRM-SCP exam.

Structure of the SHRM BASK

Simply reading through the SHRM BASK may be a daunting task due to the amount of information it contains. Before tackling the detail, it can be helpful to understand the structure and the elements comprising the model. Let's start with the basics.

> » HR technical competency; divided into three content domains: *People*, *Organization*, and *Workplace*.

> » Behavioral competency; divided into three content clusters: *Business*, *Interpersonal*, and *Leadership*.

The HR technical competency, **HR Expertise**, reflects the technical knowledge specific to the HR field for an HR professional to perform their role. **Behavioral competencies**, on the other hand, describe the knowledge, skills, abilities and other characteristics (KSAOs) that define proficient performance for a professional. They are more general in their applicability than the profession-specific technical competency. That is, many of these competencies may apply to different jobs, roles and professions but have been specifically defined in HR terms for the SHRM BASK.

In short, the HR Expertise technical competencies reflect what knowledge HR professionals apply on the job, and behavioral competencies reflect how they apply this knowledge.

Before we dig deeper, Figure 2.2 presents a high-level overview of the SHRM BASK structure including how Key Concepts (KC) or Proficiency Indicators (PI), or both, support the content area you are studying. Ensure you review the applicable Key Concepts and Proficiency Indicators, where applicable.

HR Expertise		
People	**Organization**	**Workplace**
» HR Strategy KC/PI » Talent Acquisition KC/PI » Employee Engagement & Retention KC/PI » Learning & Development KC/PI » Total Rewards KC/PI	» Structure of the HR Function KC/PI » Organizational Effectiveness & Development KC/PI » Workforce Management KC/PI » Employee & Labor Relations KC/PI » Technology Management KC/PI	» Managing a Global Workforce KC/PI » Risk Management KC/PI » Corporate Social Responsibility KC/PI » *U.S. Employment Law & Regulations KC/PI

Behavioral Competencies			
Leadership	**Leadership & Navigation KC** » Navigating the Organization PI » Vision PI » Managing HR Initiatives PI » Influence PI	**Ethical Practice KC** » Personal Integrity PI » Professional Integrity PI » Ethical Agent PI	**Inclusion & Diversity KC** » Creating an Inclusive and Diverse Culture PI » Ensuring Equity Effectiveness PI » Connecting I&D to Organizational Performance PI
Interpersonal	**Relationship Management KC** » Networking PI » Relationship Building PI » Teamwork PI » Negotiation PI » Conflict Management PI	**Communication KC** » Delivering Messages PI » Exchanging Organizational Information PI » Listening PI	**Global Mindset KC** » Operating in a Culturally Diverse Workplace PI » Operating in a Global Environment PI » Advocating for a Culturally Inclusive and Diverse Workplace PI
Business	**Business Acumen KC** » Business and Competitive Awareness PI » Business Analysis PI » Strategic Alignment PI	**Consultation KC** » Evaluating Business Challenges PI » Designing HR Solutions PI » Advising on HR Solutions PI » Change Management PI » Service Excellence PI	**Analytical Aptitude KC** » Data Advocate PI » Data Gathering PI » Data Analysis PI » Evidence-Based Decision-Making PI

U.S. Employment Law & Regulations content will only appear if you are testing within the U.S. If you are testing elsewhere across the globe, via in-person testing or report proctoring, those items will be substituted with other items from the Workplace HR Expertise domain.

Figure 2.2. Overall Structure of the SHRM BASK

HR Expertise

The HR technical competency, HR Expertise, reflects the principles, practices, and functions of effective HR management. This competency is grouped into three main knowledge domains: *People, Organization, and Workplace*. The knowledge domains are further divided into 14 HR functional knowledge areas that describe the technical knowledge required to perform key HR activities.

» **People:** HR Strategy, Talent Acquisition, Employee Engagement & Retention, Learning & Development, and Total Rewards

» **Organization:** Structure of the HR Function, Organizational Effectiveness & Development, Workforce Management, Employee & Labor Relations, and Technology Management

» **Workplace:** Managing a Global Workforce, Risk Management, Corporate Social Responsibility, and U.S. Law & Regulations

Each HR technical competency includes the following information:

» Definition of the functional area,

» Key concepts describing the knowledge specific to the functional area, and

» Proficiency indicators that apply to **All HR Professionals** (i.e., early career through executive career levels) as well as those that apply primarily to **Advanced HR Professionals** (i.e., senior and executive career levels).

> › Note that for the SHRM-SCP, proficiency indicators for All HR Professionals are the key ones to attend to.

Behavioral Competencies

Behavioral competencies facilitate the application of technical knowledge. Successful HR professionals must understand and effectively perform the behavioral components of HR practice in addition to being in command of technical HR knowledge. The nine behavioral competencies are grouped into three clusters:

» **Business**: Business Acumen, Consultation, and Analytical Aptitude

» **Interpersonal**: Relationship Management, Communication, and Global Mindset

» **Leadership**: Leadership & Navigation, Ethical Practice, and Inclusion & Diversity

Unlike the HR technical competency, each behavioral competency is further comprised of three to five sub-competencies for a total of thirty-three sub-competencies. Refer back to Figure 2.2 for an overview of the sub-competencies by their competency and cluster. For each behavioral competency, the following information is provided:

» Definition of the competency,

» Key concepts describing the foundational knowledge for the competency,

» Sub-competencies applicable to the competency, with definitions, and

» Proficiency indicators that apply to all HR professionals as well as those that apply primarily to advanced HR professionals.

> › Similarly, proficiency indicators for all HR professionals are the key ones to attend to when preparing for the SHRM-SCP exam.

Key Concepts and Proficiency Indicators

Structural Difference in the SHRM BASK

In addition to the what and how distinction between HR Expertise and behavioral competencies, another difference important to understanding the structure of the SHRM BASK focuses on where the key concepts and proficiency indicators are specified in the model.

As depicted in Figure 2.2, key concepts (KC) and proficiency indicators (PI) are specified for each knowledge area under **HR Expertise** technical competency (note the superscripts beside each knowledge area). However, behavioral competencies are structured differently in this regard: Key concepts are identified by behavioral competency, and proficiency indicators are identified by sub-competency.

The SHRM-CP certification focuses on the proficiency indicators identified for *All HR Professionals*, and the SHRM-SCP certification exam focuses only on the indicators identified for *Advanced HR Professionals*. Although the proficiency indicators relevant to all HR professionals clearly apply to advanced HR professionals at the senior and executive levels, they are not assessed directly on these indicators but are expected, on the job, to understand the concepts behind these functions, recognize their strategic importance, and be able to mentor junior employees in developing those behaviors.

Example of Parallel Proficiency Indicators

An example of this distinction can be seen by parallel proficiency indicators presented under the *Corporate Social Responsibility* (CSR) knowledge area within the Workplace functional knowledge domain.

» For **Advanced HR Professionals**: *Develops a CSR strategy that reflects the organization's mission and values.*

» For **All HR Professionals**: *Identifies and promotes opportunities for HR and the organization to engage in CSR activities that align with the organization's CSR strategy.*

Both proficiency indicators address the organization's CSR strategy. The *advanced* proficiency indicator highlights the higher-level organizational focus of developing this strategy, whereas the *all* proficiency indicator focuses on supporting the strategy by identifying and promoting opportunities in alignment with the organizational strategy.

How to Use the SHRM BASK for Studying

Now that you have an understanding of the overall structure of the SHRM BASK, the next step is to understand the format of exam items and how you can leverage the information in the SHRM BASK to help your preparation for the exam.

Item Types

Both the SHRM-CP and SHRM-SCP certification exams consist of two types of items: knowledge items (KIs)[1] and situational judgment items (SJIs).

Knowledge Items

KIs are stand-alone, multiple-choice items that test a single piece of knowledge or application of knowledge and make up 60% of the exam. Topics stem from the key concepts and proficiency indicators presented throughout the SHRM BASK.

Each KI assesses content knowledge according to one of four possible cognitive classifications, or levels of understanding or application, required to answer it:

» **Recall** items test the facts for that key concept such as defining a specific term or identifying a component of a theoretical model. This is the most basic type of KI.

» **Understanding** items requires the test taker to demonstrate their content knowledge by comprehending information, comparing two things, translating by applying knowledge or interpreting a concept to apply it to an example. These items assess the test taker's ability to recognize how HR concepts and terms manifest themselves in the workplace.

» **Problem-solving** items require test takers to apply their knowledge to develop a solution to a problem, which is something HR professionals do every day. To select the correct answer, the test taker must draw on their knowledge and understanding of many different concepts and strategies, which is more cognitively demanding than simply recalling the information.

» **Critical evaluation** items ask test takers to analyze information to predict an outcome. A competent HR professional uses the ability to predict outcomes to guide business strategy and execution.

Situational Judgement Items

In comparison, SJIs test decision-making and judgment skills to identify the most effective response according to HR best practices, as established by HR subject matter experts. These items make up 40% of the exam, and involve three major components:

» A realistic situation (scenario) that is similar to what many HR professionals have likely experienced during their careers,

---

1.   The *Ace Your SHRM Certification Exam: The Official SHRM Study Guide for the SHRM-CP and SHRM-SCP Exams* references two types of knowledge items: KIs and foundational KIs (FKIs). KIs and FKIs follow the same structure; the only meaningful difference is that the content for a KI stem from a knowledge area under *HR Expertise,* whereas the content for an FKI stem from a *behavioral competency.* For this workbook, we refer to all knowledge items as KIs.

» Two to three questions addressing the scenario prompting test takers to solve a particular situation-specific issue in an action-oriented way, and

» Four possible response options.

For example, while a KI may test your knowledge about different communication elements or techniques (for example, under the *Communication* behavioral competency), an SJI may ask you to identify the most effective way to communicate with leaders or with the organization given the circumstances presented in the scenario. In lieu of being able to assess each test taker's real-life response to the same situation, an SJI offers an opportunity for test takers to leverage their knowledge of key concepts, as well as HR best practices, to demonstrate how they might have responded to a similar real-life situation.

For more information about these item types, please refer to the SHRM Learning System or *Ace Your SHRM Certification Exam.*

Creating a Study Guide from the SHRM BASK

As noted previously, simply reading the SHRM BASK may be overwhelming and, as a result, not particularly helpful as a test preparation approach. Rather, the model needs to be consumed in smaller bites. In the remainder of this section, we present an approach to examining the different components of the SHRM BASK to identify particular topics to study and further investigate during your test preparation.

First, we recommend picking a knowledge area or behavioral competency and sub-competency as a starting point. From there, you will leverage the key concepts and proficiency indicators to support the development of your customized study guide. You will repeat these steps for each knowledge area and sub-competency until you have completed your review of the SHRM BASK.

We present examples of applying this approach to a knowledge area and a behavioral competency and sub-competency in Section 3.

How to Study Key Concepts

Key concepts are the most straightforward component of the SHRM BASK with respect to identifying information to build your study guide. They specify the complete list of topics that will be covered on both the SHRM-CP and SHRM-SCP exams. Figuring out what you need to know and what is tested on the exam is an excellent place to start.

How to Study Proficiency Indicators

Proficiency indicators are a bit more complicated to use for building a study guide. They require more self-reflection and analysis than key concepts. As noted previously, proficiency indicators reflect what competent HR behavior and performance look like in practice. That is, they define high-level HR best practices according to their associated knowledge area or behavioral sub-competency. We present some recommended steps to analyze a proficiency indicator to help build your study guide.

Before we get started, you need to be clear which exam you are preparing for: SHRM-CP or SHRM-SCP. Remember that proficiency indicators are differentiated by which exam you will take. Indicators for all HR professionals will be assessed on the SHRM-CP exam, whereas indicators for advanced HR professionals will be assessed on the SHRM-SCP exam.

Important Reminder

When reviewing the SHRM BASK, it is important to remember that the competency model reflects expectations for the HR profession in general and not your specific HR role or those of others in your organization. It is easy to get confused about what you do (or have done) in your career and what is considered proficient for the HR professional at your level in general.

Depending on your current job and past experiences, you may not have had the opportunity to perform or experience everything specified in the SHRM BASK, and that is okay. You don't have to have experience in all the areas presented to be eligible to take the exam. They are a guide as to what is expected of an HR professional at your level.

QUICK TIP
Recommended Steps to Identifying Key Concepts to Study

1. Review the list of key concepts for the particular functional knowledge area or behavioral competency of interest.

2. Ask yourself the following questions:

    » Which concepts do I know extremely well?

    » Which concepts am I only familiar with at a superficial level?

    » Which concepts do I have limited to no knowledge about?

3. Take note of with which key concepts you have only some or no famil-iarity. These are good targets to add to your study guide. It can also be useful to refresh on the key concepts that you think you know extremely well.

4. Think about how the key concept could be tested with KIs, according to the four cognitive levels (i.e., recall, understanding, problem-solving, and critical evaluation).

    » What are the facts about this key concept?

    » How would I demonstrate understanding of this key concept?

    » What types of problems could I be expected to solve that would rely on this key concept?

    » Can I predict outcomes under varying conditions?

QUICK TIP
Recommended Steps to Understanding Proficiency Indicators for the SHRM-SCP exam

1. Review the proficiency indicators for *All HR Professionals* for a particular knowledge area or behavioral sub-competency of interest.

2. Ask yourself the following questions:

   » Which indicators resonate with experiences I have had during my HR career?

   » Which indicators am I familiar with because I have observed others perform them?

   » Which indicators am I unfamiliar with altogether?

3. As you did with the key concepts, take note of which proficiency indicators fall into each category. They will all require some further analysis to support your test preparation.

4. For each proficiency indicator, think about which key concepts are valuable for supporting the proficient performance of this indicator. Linking key concepts to proficiency indicators can aid your understanding of different applications for a key concept and scenarios you could encounter on the exam in KIs and SJIs.

5. For each proficiency indicator, identify the HR best practices for this indicator.

   » Think about what steps are involved in satisfying the proficiency indicator.

   » Identify any additional key concepts that you didn't initially select that could now be useful to study more closely. Go back to the recommended steps for using key concepts to determine if these need to go on your study guide list.

   » Consider that you may know the ways that you have handled this proficiency indicator in the past and these responses may have been effective for your given situation, but they may not actually reflect HR best practices.

   » Take note of the situations you have encountered or witnessed that have involved this proficiency indicator as these could be reflected on the exam.

   » Identify and add any HR best practices and proficiency indicators to your study guide list.

   » Can I predict outcomes under varying conditions?

Section 3

Using the SHRM BASK to Prepare for the SHRM-SCP Exam

In this section, we take what we learned in Section 2 and apply it to the HR Expertise areas and behavioral competencies, selecting an example of each to highlight how you can leverage the SHRM BASK in your test preparation. This process will help you figure out what you need to study and understand the nuance underlying the SHRM BASK.

HR Expertise Example: Structure of the HR Function

Using the recommended steps presented in Section 2, let's go through an example using the **Structure of the HR Function** knowledge area within the **Organization** knowledge domain. This technical knowledge area encompasses the people, processes and activities involved in the delivery of HR-related services that create and drive organizational effectiveness. Note that the material presented under the HR Expertise technical competency will only be assessed with KIs.

Note that the material presented under the HR Expertise technical competency will only be assessed with KIs.

Key Concepts

Because key concepts define testable content material, especially for KIs, we will start here and then move to proficiency indicators, selecting one example of each to examine more closely.

Step 1. Review Key Concepts

The first step is the most basic: Read the list of key concepts and the examples associated with the concepts. The key concepts for *Structure of the HR Function* are as follows:

» Approaches to HR function and service models;

» Approaches to HR structural models;

» Elements of the HR function;

» HR staff roles, responsibilities, and functions;

» Outsourcing of HR functions; and

» HR-function metrics.

Step 2. Categorize Key Concepts According to Level of Familiarity

For each key concept, categorize them according to familiarity: extremely familiar, somewhat familiar (i.e., superficial knowledge), and limited to no familiarity. Make sure to review the associated examples as there may be some for which you may have more or less knowledge.

Step 3. Take Note of Any Key Concepts Requiring Additional Study

Any key concepts that fall into the latter two categories of somewhat or no familiarity are targets for further investigation and study. Identify these topics for your personal study guide. Recognize, of course, that a refresher review of any key concepts that you are already very comfortable with is a good idea to ensure your knowledge is up to date with the literature.

For this example, we will select the key concept—**elements of the HR function**.

> » Examples of this key concept include *recruiting, talent management, compensation,* and *benefits.*

Step 4. Identify How the Key Concept May Be Assessed with a KI

When studying the various key concepts, it is easy to stick to learning the facts about the concept such as the details associated with a particular theory or the steps involved in a process. Think about how you might use your knowledge to demonstrate your understanding, and ability to solve situational problems, or predict outcomes.

Returning to our example, how might *elements of the HR function* be tested with a stand-alone KI?

To demonstrate how group dynamics can be assessed differently, Figures 3.1 and 3.2 present example KIs that reflect understanding and problem-solving, respectively.

Although both KI examples address elements of the HR function concepts, the recall item straightforwardly focuses on the definition of key terminology and does not require the test taker to do anything further than remember the information. The problem-solving KI, on the other hand, requires the test taker to take what they know about elements of the HR function and identify an effective solution to achieve the desired result of supporting the staffing of the new branch.

| What is characterized by the measurement of employee behavior, employee turnover, and organizational performance?

A.　Employee engagement

B.　Career management

C.　Job withdrawal

D.　Performance management | **Key:** A, Employee Engagement

Description: This item requires the test taker to recall the definition of employee engagement to select the correct answer. Employee engagement is a measure of an individual's involvement in, satisfaction with, and enthusiasm for the work they are performing. A higher level of employee engagement has been shown in studies to affect customer satisfaction, company profit levels, employee turnover, and on-the-job accidents. |

Figure 3.1. Recall KI for Elements of the HR Function

A department store chain is opening a new branch. The HR manager needs to hire 100 store assistants to start operations in three months. What is the best approach to ensure the store is appropriately staffed?

A. Engage the total rewards manager to work with recruiters for quick decisions on offers for successful candidates.

B. Assign HR team members to partner with line managers to lead recruiting and training locally at the new store.

C. Send the HR manager on a temporary assignment to manage the recruitment activities at the new store.

D. Meet with the VP of HR to discuss the risks associated with the compressed hiring timeline.

Key: B, Assign HR team members to partner with line managers to lead recruiting and training locally at the new store.

Description: This item is classified as problem-solving because it asks the test taker to assess the situation presented in the item and identify the best course of action given knowledge of elements of the HR function. Assigning an HR team member to partner with the line managers of the new branch is considered a best practice as it builds the local skillset to support future recruitment and training, while ensuring the ability to onboard a large number of new employees in a short amount of time.

Figure 3.2. Problem-Solving KI Elements for the HR Function

Proficiency Indicators

Proficiency indicators reflect HR best practices related to the HR technical competency or behavioral sub-competencies and can best be leveraged to identify context for situational prompts. As noted previously, they tend to be defined at the highest level of proficiency without dictating how the action can be accomplished. As a result, further analysis is required to support building a personal study guide.

Let's continue with our example of the functional knowledge area of *Structure of the HR Function* and apply the recommended process for one proficiency indicator.

Step 1. Review Proficiency Indicators for All HR Professionals

For the SHRM-SCP exam, review the proficiency indicators listed for *Advanced HR Professionals*. The proficiency indicators for *Structure of the HR Function* are as follows:

» Designs, implements and adjusts the HR service model for the organization to ensure efficient and effective delivery of services to stakeholders.

» Creates long-term goals and implements changes that address feedback from stakeholders identifying opportunities for HR function improvements.

» Ensures that all elements of the HR function are aligned and integrated, and that they provide timely and consistent delivery of services to stakeholders.

» Identifies opportunities to improve HR operations by outsourcing work or implementing technologies that automate HR functions.

» Designs and oversees programs to collect, analyze and interpret HR-function metrics to evaluate the effectiveness of HR activities in supporting organizational success.

Step 2. Categorize Proficiency Indicators According to Level of Familiarity

For each proficiency indicator, ask yourself the following questions regarding your familiarity with them as a result of your HR career to date:

» Which indicators resonate with experiences I have had during my HR career? (Extremely Familiar)

» Which indicators am I only familiar with because I have observed others perform them? (Somewhat Familiar)

» Which indicators am I unfamiliar with altogether? (Limited to No Familiarity)

Categorize the indicators according to familiarity: extremely familiar, somewhat familiar (i.e., superficial knowledge), and limited to no familiarity.

Step 3. Take Note of Any Proficiency Indicators Requiring Additional Study

Take note of which proficiency indicators fall into each familiarity category. Unlike key concepts, they will all require further analysis to support your test preparation.

Step 4. Link Proficiency Indicators to Key Concepts

For each proficiency indicator, think about which key concepts are valuable for supporting the proficient performance of this proficiency indicator. Linking key concepts to proficiency indicators can aid your understanding of different applications for a key concept and scenarios you could encounter on the exam.

For example, let's look at the indicator, *ensures that all elements of the HR function are aligned and integrated, and that they provide timely and consistent delivery of services to stakeholders.* What key concepts are relevant to this indicator?

» *Approaches to HR function/service models* because understanding different approaches and service models is essential to ensuring that the approach supports timely and consistent delivery of services,

» *Approaches to HR structural models* because understanding these models is essential to ensuring the right model for the organization is in place,

» *Elements of the HR function* because these features are the foundation to the HR function, and

» *HR staff roles, responsibilities and function* because understanding this concept will enable strategic allocation of resources to support effective service delivery.

The problem-solving KI example presented in Figure 3.2 effectively demonstrates how a proficiency indicator can be leveraged to identify a context for applying a key concept. For convenience, we re-present the stem with an explanation of the linkage in Figure 3.3.

Item Stem	Linkage Explanation
A department store chain is opening a new branch. The HR manager needs to hire 100 store assistants to start operations in three months. What is the best approach to ensure the store is appropriately staffed?	The item presents a situation and asks the test taker to recommend an approach to supporting the recruitment and onboarding of a large number of staff in a short period of time. This item requires knowledge of the key concept (*elements of the HR function*) and directly links to the proficiency indicator (*ensures that all elements of the HR function are aligned and integrated, and that they provide timely and consistent delivery of services to stakeholders*).

Figure 3.3. Key Concept Linkage Example: Technical Knowledge Area Proficiency Indicator

Step 5. Identify HR Best Practices

As written, there is a great deal of nuance in how a proficiency indicator can be accomplished or performed. Each proficiency indicator, as a result, can be broken down into lower-level components, each of which may have their own set of recommended best practices. Examining the lower-level steps or components will help you identify additional contextual situations that you may encounter on the exam, as well as additional key concepts that you may need to consider for review.

For each proficiency indicator

1. Think about how this proficiency indicator can be accomplished. What steps, factors, or other considerations are involved in satisfying the proficiency indicator?

   For this example indicator (*ensures that all elements of the HR function are aligned and integrated, and that they provide timely and consistent delivery of services to stakeholders*), factors to consider might include organizational and HR function metrics, feedback from stakeholders, outsourcing opportunities, workflow processes, or intended and unintended consequences to processes.

2. Identify any additional key concepts that you didn't initially select that could now be useful. Go back to the recommended steps for using key concepts to determine if these need to go on your study guide list.

   For example, if a lower-level step involves evaluating different service models to improve service delivery, you may want to add the key concept, **outsourcing of HR functions**, to your list of key concepts to study (if you haven't already).

3. Consider that you may know the ways that you have handled this proficiency indicator in the past and these responses may have been effective for your given situation, but they may not actually reflect HR best practices.

4. Take note of the situations you have encountered or witnessed that have involved this proficiency indicator as these could be reflected on the exam.

5. Identify and add any HR best practices and proficiency indicators to your study guide list as needed.

Behavioral Competency Example: Relationship Management

Now let's do the same thing using a behavioral competency as the starting point, using *Relationship Management* from the *Interpersonal* cluster. Relationship Management is defined as the KSAOs needed to create and maintain a network of professional contacts within and outside the organization, to build and maintain relationships, to work as an effective member of a team, and to manage conflict while supporting the organization.

As evident in Figure 2.2, key concepts are specified at the behavioral competency level. As a result, we will begin with the behavioral competency when reviewing key concepts and eventually narrow down to a sub-competency when examining the proficiency indicators.

Key Concepts

As we did for HR Expertise, we will present how to use the recommended approach, focusing on one key concept for demonstration.

Step 1. Review Key Concepts

Read the list of key concepts and the examples associated with the concepts. The key concepts for *Relationship Management* are as follows:

» Types of conflict;

» Conflict resolution strategies;

» Negotiation tactics, strategies, and styles; and

» Trust-building techniques.

Step 2. Categorize Key Concepts According to Level of Familiarity

For each key concept, categorize them according to familiarity: extremely familiar, somewhat familiar (i.e., superficial knowledge), and limited to no familiarity. Make sure to review the associated examples as there may be some for which you may have more or less knowledge.

Step 3. Take Note of Any Key Concepts Requiring Additional Study

Any key concepts that fall into the latter two categories of somewhat or no familiarity are targets for further investigation and study. Identify these topics for your personal study guide. Recognize, of course, that a refresher review of any key concepts that you are already very comfortable with is a good idea to ensure your knowledge is up to date with the literature.

For this example, we will select the key concept of *conflict resolution strategies*. Examples of this key concept include accommodation, collaboration, compromise, competition, and avoidance.

Step 4. Identify How the Key Concept May Be Assessed with a KI

Think about how you might use your knowledge to demonstrate your understanding and ability to solve situational problems, or predict outcomes.

Returning to our example, how might *conflict resolution strategies* be tested with a stand-alone KI?

To demonstrate how conflict resolution strategies can be assessed differently, Figures 3.4 and 3.5 present examples of KIs that reflect understanding and problem-solving, respectively.

Although both KI examples address conflict resolution strategies and present example situations, the understanding item asks the test taker to assess the example and identify the term reflected in the example. The problem-solving KI, on the other hand, requires the test taker to take what they know about conflict resolution strategies and identify an effective solution to achieve the desired result of resolving the finance manager's frustrations.

Proficiency Indicators

Continuing with *Relationship Management*, let's look at the proficiency indicators and follow the recommended approach identified in Section 2. However, as noted previously, remember that proficiency indicators are specified under sub-competencies. For this exercise, we will focus on the sub-competency of *Conflict Management*, which focuses on the management and resolution of conflicts by identifying areas of common interest among the parties in conflict.

Which conflict-resolution style is most appropriate to find a temporary solution between groups who have opposite goals but equal power?	**Key**: C, Compromising
A. Integrating B. Obliging C. Compromising D. Dominating	**Description**: This item requires the test taker to use their knowledge of *conflict resolution strategies* and assess which style would achieve the desired result. The compromising resolution strategy focuses on finding a mutually agreeable solution that satisfies both parties and is considered the most effective to support an initial temporary solution until a more permanent solution can be achieved. Integrating strategy can also effectively bring both parties together but can be more time-consuming. The other two strategies balance the other party's needs against one's own and would not be effective for a temporary solution.

Figure 3.4. Understanding KI for Conflict Resolution Strategies

The finance manager expresses disappointment over a project that was launched by the HR department. Which approach should the HR manager take to resolve the finance manager's frustrations? A. Discuss with the finance manager solutions or alternatives to the project. B. Create a response to answer any questions about the benefits of the project. C. Explain that in making the decision, the department was aware that not all employees would agree with the project. D. Ask the finance manager to document suggestions for project improvements.	**Key:** A, Discuss with the finance manager solutions or alternatives to the project. **Description:** This item requires that the test taker assess the situation presented and identify the best course of action given knowledge of *conflict resolution strategies*. Engaging in a discussion with the finance manager is considered an effective best practice because, unlike the other options, it involves a dialog and allows the HR manager to better understand the finance manager's issues to help reach a resolution.

Figure 3.5. Problem-Solving KI for Conflict Resolution Strategies

Step 1. Review Proficiency Indicators for All HR Professionals

For the SHRM-SCP exam, review the proficiency indicators listed for *Advanced HR Professionals*. The proficiency indicators for *Conflict Management* are as follows:

» Designs and oversees conflict resolution strategies and processes throughout the organization.

» Facilitates difficult interactions among senior leaders to achieve optimal outcomes.

» Identifies and reduces potential sources of conflict when proposing new HR strategies or initiatives.

» Mediates or resolves escalated conflicts.

Step 2. Categorize Proficiency Indicators According to Level of Familiarity

For each proficiency indicator, ask yourself the following questions regarding your familiarity with them as a result of your HR career to date:

» Which indicators resonate with experiences I have had during my HR career? (Extremely Familiar)

» Which indicators am I only familiar with because I have observed others perform them? (Somewhat Familiar)

» Which indicators am I unfamiliar with altogether? (Limited to No Familiarity)

Categorize the indicators according to familiarity: extremely familiar, somewhat familiar (i.e., superficial knowledge), and limited to no familiarity.

Step 3. Take Note of Any Proficiency Indicators Requiring Additional Study

Take note of which proficiency indicators fall into each familiarity category. Unlike for key concepts, they will all require further analysis to support your test preparation.

Step 4. Link Proficiency Indicators to Key Concepts

For each proficiency indicator, think about which key concepts are valuable for supporting the proficient performance of this indicator. Linking key concepts to proficiency indicators can aid your understanding of different applications for a key concept and scenarios you could encounter on the exam.

For the indicator, **facilitates difficult interactions among senior leaders to achieve optimal outcomes**, for example, what key concepts are relevant to this indicator?

» *Types of conflict* because knowing the type of conflict may impact which strategies should be considered,

» *Conflict resolution strategies* because this indicator clearly focuses on designing processes in alignment with conflict resolution strategies, and

» *Trust-building techniques* because effective conflict resolution typically involves employing the techniques presented as examples.

The problem-solving KI example presented in Figure 3.5 effectively demonstrates how a proficiency indicator can be leveraged to identify a context for applying a key concept. For convenience, we re-present the stem with an explanation of the linkage in Figure 3.6.

Behavioral sub-competency proficiency indicators can also provide situational context for SJIs. The next examples (Figure 3.7) showcase two SJIs based on the same scenario, both focusing on the sub-competency, Conflict Management.

Item Stem	Linkage Explanation
The finance manager expresses disappointment over a project that was launched by the HR department. Which approach should the HR manager take to resolve the finance manager's frustrations?	The item presents a situation and asks the test taker to recommend a conflict resolution approach to address the finance manager's frustration with a new HR initiative. This item requires knowledge of the key concept (conflict resolution strategies) and directly links to the proficiency indicator (facilitates difficult interactions among senior leaders to achieve optimal outcomes).

Figure 3.6. Key Concept Linkage Example: Sub-Competency Proficiency Indicator

SJI Scenario
A manager approaches the HR director asking for assistance in resolving a conflict between two high-performing employees who report to the manager. One employee is less tenured, and the other employee has worked for the company for several years. The less-tenured employee complains that the long-tenured employee is very rude whenever he asks for information. As a result, this has made him unwilling to ask for assistance. The long-tenured employee, on the other hand, claims that the less-tenured employee is overreacting and that their relationship is fine. Meanwhile, clients have begun to complain about the two employees regarding a decrease in productivity, and a decline in customer service ratings. The manager has been unable to resolve the conflict and has asked the HR director to intervene.

Conflict Management SJI 1	
Which action should the HR director take to resolve the conflict between the employees? A. Listen to each employee separately and suggest a solution to the manager. B. Partner with the manager to facilitate a mediation session between the employees. C. Require both employees to attend a conflict resolution training course. D. Meet with each employee separately to provide coaching on handling the situation.	**Key:** B, Partner with the manager to facilitate a mediation session between the employees.

Conflict Management SJI 2	
The HR director has noticed that conflicts between employees have been increasing across the company and that managers have been asking HR to intervene without actively trying to resolve the conflicts on their own. What should the HR director do to help managers handle employee conflicts? A. Send an email to all managers providing suggestions on resolving conflicts between employees. B. Create conflict resolution training for new managers entering the company. C. Provide conflict resolution training to all managers in the company. D. Require managers to document all steps they have taken before bringing an issue to HR.	**Key:** C, Provide conflict resolution training to all managers in the company.

Figure 3.7. SJIs for Conflict Management

Step 5. Identify HR Best Practices

This step is focused on doing a deeper dive into understanding the best practices associated with a proficiency indicator. Doing this analysis will help you identify additional contextual situations that you may encounter on the exam, as well as additional key concepts that you may need to consider for additional review.

For each proficiency indicator

1. Think about how this proficiency can be accomplished. What steps, factors, or other considerations are involved in satisfying the proficiency indicator?

    For example, the indicator (designs and oversees conflict resolution strategies and processes throughout the organization) may involve considering factors such as organizational culture, existing policies and procedures, existing training and development opportunities, results from investigations, and stakeholder feedback.

2. Identify any additional key concepts that you didn't initially select that could now be useful. Go back to the recommended steps for using key concepts to determine if these need to go on your study guide list.

    For example, your initial review of the proficiency indicator may not have signaled that designing and overseeing conflict resolution strategies and processes throughout the organization could require negotiation tactics but now you do. Therefore, you may want to add the key concept (negotiation tactics, strategies, and styles) to your list of key concepts to study (if you haven't already).

3. Consider that you may know the ways that you have handled this proficiency indicator in the past and these responses may have been effective for your given situation, but they may not actually reflect HR best practices.

4. Take note of the situations you have encountered of witnessed that have involved this proficiency indicator as these could be reflected on the exam.

5. Identify and add any HR best practices and proficiency indicators to your study guide list, as needed.

Let's Practice! Twenty SHRM-SCP Practice Items and Answers

Now, let's apply what we have learned over the past two sections regarding the use of the SHRM BASK as a preparation tool combined with this set of twenty practice items. Each of these items was previously administered on the SHRM-SCP exam as a scored test item. This practice item list is not reflective of the entire blueprint that is used to build the SHRM-SCP exams. In other words, these practice items are not a mini-exam, and they do not represent all knowledge or behavioral areas tested on the exams.

Separated by item type:

» **Section 1** contains a total of six KIs and foundational knowledge items,

» **Section 2** section contains eight SJIs, and

» **Section 3** section contains another set of six KIs and foundational knowledge items.

The items will give you a flavor of how the questions are structured on the exam and allow you to practice your testing-taking strategies as you answer them. Additionally, you will see how items are linked to the SHRM BASK, difficulty rating, and the answer key and rationale accompanying the items.

Later in this book, you will have access to an additional set of fifty SHRM-SCP KIs and SJIs for practice. This set of items will not initially include the SHRM BASK linkage, difficulty rating, or answer keys. The purpose of these items is to test yourself as if the items were actual test items. The SHRM BASK alignment, difficulty ratings, answer key responses, and rationales will be provided following the fifty practice items.

One very important caution: do not assume that the ability to answer this set of fifty practice items correctly equates to a passing score on the certification exam. Similarly, do not use the results to predict how well you will do on the certification exam itself. Combined, these lists compose just over half of the number of items on the SHRM-SCP exam. Also, these practice items do not fully cover all of the competency clusters and knowledge domains that are represented on the real exams. For these reasons, the practice items are intended to give a preview of the structure and format of test questions. It is not appropriate to use results to predict an outcome on your exam, and doing well on these practice items will not guarantee a passing result on your exam.

For examinees who plan to test outside of the United States, you will see questions about U.S. Employment Law & Regulations. Questions in this functional area do not appear on exams for examinees who reside outside of the United States. If you reside outside the United States and plan to take your exam outside of the United States, omit these questions and adjust your timing accordingly.

Section 1: This section has six knowledge items (KIs).

1. Which strategy will most effectively increase participation in a company's community volunteer program?

    A. Communicate to employees the public perception benefit to the company when they volunteer.

    B. Post volunteer activity options on workforce bulletin boards to encourage participation.

    C. Convey the positive impact of volunteerism to participants and recipients of the activities.

    D. Advertise to the public the outcomes of the company's volunteer program participation.

Domain	Sub-Competency	Difficulty	Key
Workplace	Corporate Social Responsibility	Easy	C
Rationale			
"Convey the positive impact of volunteerism to participants and recipients of the activities" is correct because identifying and communicating the benefit of volunteerism to both the employee and the recipients of the efforts decreases the possible negative connotation of corporate self-interest, and increases employee participation.			

2. Which information should an HR manager present to the CEO to most effectively improve the strategic planning process?

    A. Explain how HR can act as a mediator to help identify potential threats, obstacles, and weaknesses.

    B. Suggest that the individuals involved in the process are less important than the process itself.

    C. Propose that strategic planning occurs among high-level employees who have the most expertise.

    D. Explain how successful strategic plans depend on effective HR allocation.

Domain	Sub-Competency	Difficulty	Key
People	HR Strategy	Somewhat Hard	D
Rationale			
"Explain how successful strategic plans depend on effective HR allocation" is correct because HR planning is a critical element of a company's ability to achieve its business plans. Management's appreciation for the ways its HR decisions affect the company's bottom line is highly correlated with a company's likelihood of success.			

3. A company with locations across the country needs to improve the efficiency and delivery of its HR services. Each location has a dedicated HR generalist, and there is a small team of experts at headquarters. Which is the most effective approach to reorganizing the HR function?

   A. Ask each HR generalist to volunteer for a team that specializes in delivering one aspect of HR services.

   B. Eliminate HR representation at each location then combine HR staff into a national service center.

   C. Develop a pilot program that establishes a shared services model with HR business representation for one region.

   D. Conduct a companywide survey to collect suggestions to benchmark the HR staff's effectiveness.

Domain	Sub-Competency	Difficulty	Key
Organization	Structure of the HR Function	Somewhat Easy	C

Rationale
"Develop a pilot program that establishes a shared services model with HR business representation for one region" is correct because the firm needs to develop a proof of concept for major changes in the HR function that is then piloted extensively before implementation.

4. Which advantage does the avoidance conflict resolution strategy provide?

   A. Places responsibility directly on the team to manage their time.

   B. Allows for time to address the situation when most productive.

   C. Focuses attention on priorities and immediate results needed.

   D. Provides an environment open to celebrating personal occasions.

Domain	Sub-Competency	Difficulty	Key
Interpersonal	Relationship Management	Hard	B

Rationale
"Allows for time to address the situation when most productive" is correct because the avoidance conflict resolution strategy includes the concept of confronting the situation at the right time and place.

5. An employee of a company with 35 employees wishes to use FMLA leave to care for his seriously ill child. This employee worked 30 hours per week for the past 12 months. Based on these circumstances, what is the employee's eligibility status for FMLA leave?

    A. The employee is eligible for FMLA leave because the employee is caring for a child.

    B. The employee is ineligible for FMLA leave because he is employed on a part-time basis.

    C. The employee is ineligible for FMLA leave due to the size of the company.

    D. The employee is ineligible for FMLA leave because he did not work the yearly minimum amount of hours.

Domain	Sub-Competency	Difficulty	Key
Workplace	U.S. Employment Law & Regulations	Somewhat Easy	C
Rationale			

"The employee is ineligible for FMLA leave due to the size of the company" is correct because FMLA only applies to employers with 50 or more employees.

6. The HR department of a manufacturing organization announces a competition to solve a production problem. The competition winners are offered employment. What selection method is the organization adopting?

    A. Cognitive ability test

    B. Assessment center

    C. Work sample

    D. Situational interview

Domain	Sub-Competency	Difficulty	Key
People	Talent Acquisition	Hard	C
Rationale			

"Work sample" is correct because the competition is simulating the job situations and observing how the applicant performs in the simulated environment.

Section 2: This section has eight situational judgment items (SJIs).

The following scenario accompanies the next three items.

The results of an annual employee survey at a large software company reveal that the corporate quarterly employee reward and recognition program is perceived to be unfair by a high percentage of employees throughout the company. The program is intended to recognize high-performing employees nominated by their managers each quarter and provide the nominated employees with a monetary bonus as a reward. Employees feel as though winners are not selected based on performance but rather because they are well-liked by their managers. This negative perception is bringing down the morale of top-performing employees and creating a sense of entitlement among those who are repeatedly nominated. The CEO asks the HR director to improve the fairness perceptions and morale within the company.

7. Which action should the HR director take to investigate whether the employee perceptions of unfairness in the reward nominations are true?

    A. Review all employees' performance appraisal data to determine if previous award winners are also top performers.

    B. Ask the managers who nominated previous winners why they nominated those employees.

    C. Survey the previous winners on how likely they think it is that they will be nominated again.

    D. Request employees to identify specific cases of unfairness and investigate those cases.

Domain	Sub-Competency	Difficulty	Key
Business	Analytical Aptitude	Somewhat Easy	A

8. The HR director learns that some managers nominated employees they feared would leave the company if they did not receive a bonus, and others nominated lower performers out of fear that not nominating anyone would result in losing the reward budget for future years. Which approach should the HR director take to solve the problem of misuse of the reward program?

    A. Conduct yearly mandatory training regarding the criteria for nominating employees.

    B. Work with managers to develop a separate intervention to address employee turnover.

    C. Explain to managers that not nominating employees will not hurt their performance budget.

    D. Revise then rebrand the program to include clearer guidelines, goals, and documentation.

Domain	Sub-Competency	Difficulty	Key
Leadership	Leadership & Navigation	Easy	D

9. The CEO is concerned that the program only recognizes a select few employees each quarter and that other employees may feel neglected. Which suggestion should the HR director make to motivate all employees in the company?

    A. Suggest to the CEO that the company allow all managers to treat employees to lunch on their birthdays.

    B. Develop a recognition board on the company's website where employees can publicly post about one another's successes.

    C. Recommend increasing the frequency of the program from quarterly to biweekly.

    D. Require that managers find ways to recognize the performance of every employee.

Domain	Sub-Competency	Difficulty	Key
Business	Consultation	Somewhat Hard	B

The following scenario accompanies the next two items.

A large multinational company hired a new HR director five months ago to head one of its large-country operations. This was the first time an individual from outside the company has been appointed to the HR role, and the new HR director came from a different industry with a very different culture. After a short time in the role, the HR director begins making negative comments regarding the company's talent, culture, and policies. The comments quickly circulate among employees and, as a result, morale across the company decreases. Additionally, in the last three months, 60% of the HR director's direct reports have resigned. The corporate leadership for the country's operations decides that something must be done and asks the chief human resource officer (CHRO) to address the problem.

10. The CHRO is not familiar with the informal work roles and relationships within the HR director's business unit. How should the CHRO obtain this information about the unit?

    A. Interview the operations leader in that country to understand the informal roles and relationships.

    B. Contact the direct reports who resigned to ask them to provide details about the informal roles and relationships.

    C. Request documentation from the HR director regarding the roles and relationships among the HR staff, both formal and informal.

    D. Recommend to corporate leadership to obtain an outside consultant to meet with employees and evaluate the situation.

Domain	Sub-Competency	Difficulty	Key
Leadership	Leadership & Navigation	Somewhat Hard	A

11. The CHRO confronts the HR director about making negative comments regarding the company's talent, culture, and policies, and the HR director accuses the CHRO of trying to restrict their autonomy. How should the CHRO address the HR director's frustration while also improving the company's current situation?

    A. Give the HR director a probationary period with no intervention to see if conditions improve.

    B. Hire an executive coach to provide guidance and feedback to the HR director on dealing with the current challenges.

    C. Find the HR director another role within the organization based on the HR director's preferences.

    D. Ask the HR director what modifications should be made in the company then work with the director to implement the changes.

Domain	Sub-Competency	Difficulty	Key
Interpersonal	Relationship Management	Somewhat Hard	B

The following scenario accompanies the next three items.

A large municipal organization is dealing with challenges within its leadership. The members of the leadership team spread rumors about each other and frequently belittle other members of the leadership team in discussions overheard by direct reports. The various units within the organization are reluctant to collaborate, and the leaders are sabotaging the projects of other units to make the leaders of those units look bad. This causes the various leaders' direct reports to frequently argue, resulting in poor internal customer service with employees refusing to help others. Many blame the organization's director for the problems, claiming that the director provides no clear direction to the organization. The chief human resource officer (CHRO) decides that something must be done to change the situation.

12. The CHRO meets with the director to suggest changes to improve the cohesiveness and unity of the leadership team. Which recommendation should the CHRO suggest the director do first?

    A. The leadership team should openly discuss the problems between the separate units at the next leadership team meeting.

    B. A 360-degree feedback review should be conducted for everyone on the leadership team as soon as possible.

    C. The director should warn the members of the leadership team that they will be replaced if they do not start working as a cohesive team.

    D. The leadership team should be sent to a team-building retreat to improve unity and cohesiveness.

Domain	Sub-Competency	Difficulty	Key
Business	Consultation	Somewhat Hard	A

13. Of the current issues facing the organization, which should be the CHRO's primary concern regarding the long-term survival of the organization?

    A.   Rumors spreading among top leaders

    B.   The lack of collaboration among employees of each unit

    C.   The cross-unit arguing of employees

    D.   Failure of the director to set a clear leadership direction for the organization

Domain	Sub-Competency	Difficulty	Key
Business	Business Acumen	Easy	D

14. A unit leader tells an employee about plans to sabotage another project, and the employee reports it to HR. Which action should the CHRO take to prevent the sabotage while protecting the employee from repercussions for reporting?

    A.   Interview the leader to ask searching questions in an attempt to get the leader to confess to the planned sabotage.

    B.   Inform the employee that HR has a responsibility to act, which justifies confronting the leader about the planned sabotage.

    C.   Remind the employee of the company's existing policies protecting whistleblowers before confronting the leader about the planned sabotage.

    D.   Advise the employee of the company's existing policies protecting whistleblowers then interview other employees to learn if they know about the planned sabotage.

Domain	Sub-Competency	Difficulty	Key
Leadership	Ethical Practice	Somewhat Easy	C

Section 3: This section has six knowledge items (KIs).

15. An HR manager notices that over the past three years, the company's turnover rate sharply declines during October, November, and December. Which statistical method is best suited to examine this type of relationship?

    A. Correlation

    B. T-test

    C. Optimization

    D. Normal distribution

Domain	Sub-Competency	Difficulty	Key
Business	Analytical Aptitude	Easy	A

Rationale

"Correlation" is correct because correlation examines the relationship between two variables.

16. Which policy offers the best protection to safeguard confidential information against data security breaches?

    A. Conducting pre-employment screenings where new hires sign a confidentiality agreement emphasizing the importance of protecting information

    B. Prohibiting the use of personal devices' access to company data in the workplace by distributing employee-owned devices

    C. Allowing employees to use a personal device after signing an agreement giving the company permission to remotely wipe its business information from the device

    D. Providing periodic information security training to employees that focuses on identifying phishing scams and protecting portable devices

Domain	Sub-Competency	Difficulty	Key
Organization	Technology Management	Somewhat Hard	B

Rationale

"Prohibiting the use of personal devices' access to company data in the workplace by distributing employer-owned devices" is correct because these devices are the responsibility of the company to install up-to-date security protocols, limit exposure to known threats by blocking users' access when warranted, and should be retrieved at termination.

17. Which criteria are key when screening and selecting employees to place on international assignments?

    A. Language proficiency of the host country

    B. Job performance

    C. Cultural compatibility

    D. Technical skill set

Domain	Sub-Competency	Difficulty	Key
Workplace	Managing a Global Workforce	Somewhat Easy	C
Rationale			

"Cultural compatibility" is correct because it is a key determining factor for selecting employees for expatriate assignments as the employee's other skills and performance may be impacted by their ability to adapt to the host area's culture.

18. A company assesses its business strategy and realizes it must become more agile in response to changing trends and customer needs. How should the company restructure its operations to become more efficient in achieving this objective?

   A. Execute a reduction in force to make the organization less hierarchical and bureaucratic.

   B. Implement a matrix structure to enhance communication between key functions and departments.

   C. Decentralize the HR function so each part of the organization manages its employee issues.

   D. Redistribute decision-making authority throughout the organization to employees and line managers.

Domain	Sub-Competency	Difficulty	Key
Organization	Workforce Management	Hard	D
Rationale			

"Redistribute decision-making authority throughout the organization to employees and line managers" is correct because empowering employees at all levels to make pivotal decisions and shifting day-to-day decisions closer to where they directly affect operations better positions an organization to be more nimble and responsive to changes within the marketplace.

19. What is the first step in the career development planning process?

   A. Identify resources that employees need to reach their goals, including work experiences and relationships.

   B. Commit to helping employees reach specific, measurable, attainable, and timely goals.

   C. Provide assessment information to identify employees' strengths, weaknesses, interests, and values.

   D. Communicate performance evaluation so employees are included in the long-range plans of the company.

Domain	Sub-Competency	Difficulty	Key
People	Learning & Development	Somewhat Hard	C
Rationale			

"Provide assessment information to identify employees' strengths, weaknesses, interests, and values" is correct because the first step in creating a development plan is to assess the employee's current state and identify gaps preventing them from reaching their desired next steps.

20. Which is an example of a breach of privacy?

    A.   An employee notifies management after receiving unwanted behaviors from another co-worker.

    B.   An employee reports to HR that a co-worker was arrested for assault last month.

    C.   An employee tells a co-worker that another employee in the company was diagnosed with a terminal illness.

    D.   An employee informs a local reporter that another employee embezzles funds from the company.

Domain	Sub-Competency	Difficulty	Key
Leadership	Ethical Practice	Somewhat Easy	C
Rationale			

"An employee tells a co-worker that another employee in the company was diagnosed with a terminal illness" is correct because sharing another employee's personal medical information is a breach of privacy as a form of gossip, where the intent of sharing is not to assist the ailing employee.

Section 4

The SHRM-SCP Exam Blueprint

Not only does SHRM provide the potential content areas for the SHRM-SCP exam in the SHRM BASK, SHRM also provides the actual breakdown of the numbers of exam items in the different content areas (Figure 4.1).

When measuring the three clusters of behavioral competencies, the exam includes close to equal representation from the different areas:

» **Leadership**: 17% of overall exam items,

» **Business**: 16.5% of overall exam items, and

» **Interpersonal**: 16.5% of overall exam items.

In addition, for the HR knowledge domains, the People and Organization domains have more items than the Workplace domain. This difference is not surprising given the fact that Workplace only includes four functional areas, while People and Organization both include five functional areas.

» **People**: 18% of overall exam items,

» **Organization**: 18% of overall exam items, and

» **Workplace**: 14% of overall exam items.

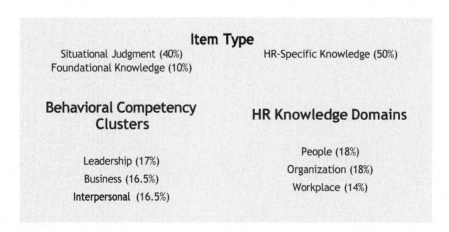

Figure 4.1. Distribution of Exam Items by Content and Exam Type

Self-Assessment for Your Exam Study Plan

Now that you have seen and started interacting with the SHRM BASK, you might feel a bit overwhelmed by the sheer volume of potential exam content. In fact, many SHRM-SCP examinees are not sure what they should spend their time focused on and where they should start studying. Remember, the SHRM Learning System is a robust option offering a comprehensive study package complete with pre-tests to assess your knowledge and identify gaps to provide a customized study plan based on your designated exam date.

To help diagnose your stronger and weaker areas and to direct your studying, we have put together this informal self-assessment for you. Note that this is not a true assessment of your knowledge but an informal resource you can use to determine where you need the most help and could benefit most in studying.

As you go through this assessment, try to be honest with yourself about your level of expertise. In many cases, you might not have a good understanding of your own knowledge level. That is okay and completely expected. If you are unsure of the meaning of terms, that is probably an indicator that you are not very knowledgeable in the area.

As a reminder, you can find the complete, complimentary, downloadable version of the SHRM BASK at

> https://www.shrm.org/credentials/certification/exam-preparation/body-of-applied-skills-and-knowledge

Instructions

Read the definition, sub-competencies (for behavioral competencies), key concepts, and proficiency indicators for all HR professionals. This will involve obtaining the full SHRM BASK and using the definitions and various pieces of information in it.

Rate the competencies and knowledge areas based on your level of expertise by placing an X in the appropriate box.

Section 1: Rate Competencies in Leadership Cluster

	Rate Your Level of Expertise		
	Low	Moderate	High
Leadership & Navigation			
Sub-competencies: » Navigating the organization » Vision » Managing HR initiatives » Influence			
Ethical Practice			
Sub-competencies: » Personal integrity » Professional integrity » Ethical agent			
Inclusion and Diversity (I&D)			
Sub-competencies: » Creating an inclusive and diverse culture » Ensuring equity effectiveness » Connecting I&D to organizational performance			

Section 2: Rate Competencies in Interpersonal Cluster

	Rate Your Level of Expertise		
	Low	Moderate	High
Relationship Management			
Sub-competencies: » Networking » Relationship building » Teamwork » Negotiation » Conflict management			
Communication			
Sub-competencies: » Delivering messages » Exchanging organizational information » Listening			
Global Mindset			
Sub-competencies: » Operating in a culturally diverse workplace » Operating in a global environment » Advocating for a culturally inclusive and diverse workplace			

Section 3: Rate Competencies in Business Cluster

	Rate Your Level of Expertise		
	Low	Moderate	High
Business Acumen			
Sub-competencies: » Business and competitive awareness » Business analysis » Strategic alignment			
Consultation			
Sub-competencies: » Evaluating business challenges » Designing HR solutions » Advising on HR solutions » Change management » Service excellence			
Analytical Aptitude			
Sub-competencies: » Data advocate » Data gathering » Data analysis » Evidence-based decision-making			

Section 4: Rate Functional Areas in People Knowledge Domain

	Rate Your Level of Expertise		
	Low	Moderate	High
HR Strategy			
Talent Acquisition			
Employee Engagement & Retention			
Learning & Development			
Total Rewards			

Section 5: Rate Functional Areas in Organization Knowledge Domain

	Rate Your Level of Expertise		
	Low	Moderate	High
Structure of the HR Function			
Organizational Effectiveness & Development			
Workforce Management			
Employee & Labor Relations			
Technology Management			

Section 6: Rate Functional Areas in Workplace Knowledge Domain

	Rate Your Level of Expertise		
	Low	Moderate	High
Managing a Global Workforce			
Risk Management			
Corporate Social Responsibility			
U.S. Employment Law & Regulations			

Scoring the Assessment

Based on your self-ratings of expertise for each behavioral competency or functional area, you can interpret the results based on your ratings of expertise.

Low Expertise = Study Most: These are areas where you have little to no expertise or experience. If you primarily support employee relations and employee engagement, you may need to study most in areas such as talent acquisition or global mindset because you have little to no hands-on experience in this area.

Moderate Expertise = Study Some: These are areas where you have some expertise or experience, but you're not an expert. This could apply if you are a generalist with experience across many (or even most) competencies; you might have a surface-level knowledge of the competency, but you need to spend some time studying to better understand that competency outside of just your role or organization. If you used to work in a specific area but now perform a different set of job duties, this might apply too.

High Expertise = Review Only: These are the areas where you have the most expertise or experience. When you create your study plan, you don't want to spend too much time on these areas. Instead, you'll devote that time to studying the areas where you have more to learn. Note that these might be areas that you prefer to study or are most comfortable with. Because of this, you might have to fight the tendency to spend too much time in areas that you already know.

Interpreting the Assessment

You should now have twenty-three discrete ratings, one for each behavioral competency and functional area. Review your ratings and make notes about the terms, facts, and concepts that you need to learn or know more about so you can include them in your study plan.

It is important to review but not overstudy areas where your knowledge and familiarity with the content is already at a command-and-control level. Instead, focus your study efforts to improve your knowledge on the content with which you are least familiar. This means you should spend the majority of your study time on your study most areas, some time on your study some areas, and only a small amount of time on your review areas. Despite these recommendations, it is also important to note that the pass/fail decision for the exams are based on overall performance, rather than performance in each specific area. As a result, it is possible to pass the exam while performing rather poorly in a small number of subject areas.

Once you have your completed self-assessment, group together the items on your checklist that you can study together to identify study blocks. As you sort items into groups, list the related terms and acronyms. Once you've identified your study blocks, you'll have the outline for your study plan.

Also, we should note that the reference list at the end of the SHRM BASK has many relevant books and other resources that are relevant for learning more about these competencies and functional areas. Remember that it is not a comprehensive list, but these are resources that have been approved by SHRM for item writers to use when creating exam items.

Create a SMART Study Plan

A plan is when a *want to* becomes a *how to*.

After going through the self-assessment and gaining some understanding of the areas of the SHRM-SCP where you might need more studying, you should commit to making a plan for preparing for the exam. Although you might be able to follow a generic or informal plan, we know that the act of planning and committing is important for a lot of people to do things that are difficult.

One of the main reasons to focus on the study plan and schedule is the importance of writing things down. You are much more likely to take a commitment more seriously if you document it in a clear way. As such, we encourage you to take advantage of this workbook and use the templates provided in Appendix 2.

Here's how to create a study schedule that will fit into your life:[1]

1. Figure out how many hours you will need to cover everything on your study checklist. SHRM research shows that you should plan on spending at least eighty hours of preparation for the exam—although some people will need significantly more preparation time.

2. Start with the results of the self-assessment and plan your study time accordingly. You should also consider factors such as the extent of your HR experience and how quickly you tend to learn.

3. Determine how much of your time is already committed elsewhere. This will vary greatly between people. You should consider the time you need for family, work, exercise, personal care, and social activities, along with downtime and time for the unexpected, such as illness or a heavier-than-usual workload.

4. Decide how many hours of study time you will have available each week before the exam. If you plan to either form or join a study group or take an exam prep course, identify how many hours each week you will need for those activities. Then divide the remaining time into study sessions.

---

1   Charles Glover, eds., *Ace Your SHRM Certification Exam: The Official SHRM Study Guide for the SHRM-CP®
and SHRM-SCP® Exams,* 3rd ed. (Alexandria, VA: SHRM, 2024), 61–63.

5. Determine a specific, achievable goal for each study session and identify the content you will study so you can achieve that goal. Keep in mind that you'll need more study time for some content than for others and build time into your schedule for practice exams so that you can assess what you are learning.

6. Develop a realistic study schedule that shows your study sessions by date and time, the goal for each session, and the content you'll focus on during that session. Try to use this to make a realistic plan for an average of six to eight hours of study per week. Please note that there is no expectation of studying every day; however, it will be a good idea for you to plan on at least three days per week of some studying.

7. Create a week-by-week calendar that includes your scheduled activities for each day during your study period. Include time for family and friends, work (including your commute), scheduled appointments (doctors, dentists, etc.), exercise, and study sessions, study group meetings, and exam prep courses (if any).

Get Started on Your Study Schedule

Now step back and review your calendar:

» How realistic is it?

» Did you leave time for meals and personal care, as well as some downtime so you can rest and relax?

» Did you leave buffer time in case of the unexpected?

If needed, go into your electronic calendar and set aside the time that you assigned to your studies.

Looking for next-level support in creating a study plan and sticking to it? As noted, the SHRM Learning System will identify strengths and gaps in knowledge, allowing more time to prioritize the studying of weaker areas, and while maintaining your areas of strength.

A great feature in the SHRM Learning System is the exam countdown calendar which will generate a customized study approach based on your selected exam date (and your proximity to it) top of mind, so you can plan your studies accordingly. You can pop in and out of the SHRM Learning System when you have a little break, using your phone to access the many quizzes and lessons within the platform.

Section 5

The SHRM-SCP Fifty-Item Practice Test

Introduction

This practice test includes fifty items that were previously used on the SHRM-SCP exam. These are different items than the ones that are used in the official SHRM study guide, *Ace Your SHRM Certification Exam*, and only include items from previous SHRM-SCP exams.

Similar to the real exam, this practice test is divided into separate sections that are composed of either knowledge items or situational judgment items.

» **Section 1** contains a total of sixteen knowledge and foundational knowledge items,

» **Section 2** contains eighteen situational judgment items, and

» **Section 3** contains another set of sixteen knowledge and foundational knowledge items.

Because this practice test only contains fifty items, it is not entirely representative of the entire blueprint that is used to build the SHRM-SCP exam. However, it is generally set up to cover all of the areas in the blueprint. This practice test will give you a taste of how the questions are structured on the exam and allow you to practice your test-taking strategies as you answer them.

To get a better sense of the real exams, SHRM recommends that you take the practice items during a timed period. We suggest you allot one and a half minutes per question (seventy-five minutes total) to gauge your ability to answer questions under the time constraints of the real exams.

One very important caution: do not assume that the ability to answer items on this fifty-item practice test directly correlates to a passing score on the certification exam. This practice test is composed of less than half of the number of items on the SHRM-SCP exam.

Additionally, the conditions in your at-home or in-office environment will not likely match the controlled environment in which a SHRM-SCP exam is administered. For these reasons, the practice items are intended to give a preview of the structure and format of test questions. It is not appropriate to use these results to predict an outcome on your exam, and doing well on the practice test is not a guarantee of a passing result on your exam.

Additional information, including the answer key and rationales for the correct answers for knowledge and foundational knowledge items, appear at the end of the practice test. Answer keys are also provided for the situational judgment items, but rationales are not provided due to the inherent nature of how these items are developed. Situational judgment items require judgment and decision-making to address workplace incidents, rather than relying on policy or law. All response options are actions that could be taken to respond to the situation, but there is only one *most effective* response. The most effective response is determined by diverse groups of experienced SHRM-certified HR professionals from around the globe who rate the effectiveness of each response. They also use the proficiency indicators outlined by the nine behavioral competencies in the SHRM BASK. Scoring the most effective response is only done if the group of HR experts agree that this is the best response of all given alternatives.

When answering the SJI questions, do not base your response on an approach that is specific to your organization. Rather, use your understanding of HR best practice, which is documented in the SHRM BASK, to select your response.

To further enhance your preparation for the exam, consider the SHRM Learning System—which includes full-length SHRM-CP and SHRM-SCP practice (timed) exams full of previously used test items along with learning modules and over 2,700 practice items to help fill in your knowledge gaps. The SHRM Learning System is offered in a variety of formats—self-study and virtual or in-person seminars—and through partner universities that are authorized to teach the SHRM Learning System content.

SHRM-SCP Practice Test Questions

Section 1: This section has sixteen knowledge items (KIs).

1. Which action should an HR manager take to best contribute to business strategy?

    A. Provide measurable, value-adding deliverables that impact company key performance indicators.

    B. Develop meaningful partnerships with key executives within the company.

    C. Focus on HR initiatives that are most important to the company's culture.

    D. Attend key strategy meetings to ensure HR initiatives are included in the business plan.

2. An employee is concerned that a promotion was denied because of their participation in a discrimination investigation involving their department manager. Which action should HR take to address this concern?

    A. Create a succession plan with input from objective stakeholders.

    B. Provide new hires with a copy of the anti-retaliation statement.

    C. Train managers on what constitutes a protected concerted activity.

    D. Implement a zero-tolerance policy for harassment by a manager.

3. What is the primary reason employers participate in salary surveys?

    A. Establish a peer group.

    B. Increase compensation for top performers.

    C. Evaluate pay based on competitors.

    D. Increase employee retention.

4. A company decides to reduce its labor expenses by running a portion of the business operations from another country and employing labor from that country. What term best describes the cost reduction strategy the company is using?

    A. Outsourcing

    B. Offshoring

    C. Temporary employees

    D. Workforce utilization review

5. Which activity provides the best chance of success for a newly formed work team?

    A. Allow team members to spend a day together doing team-building activities.

    B. Ask each team member to openly pledge commitment to achieving the team's objectives.

    C. Facilitate conversations about individual preferences on ground rules for the team's members.

    D. Conduct personality assessments to determine the best roles for team members.

6. An HR manager receives a large number of requests for more support for the company's working parents. Which step should the HR manager take first?

    A. Ask the CEO what resources are available for parental support programs.

    B. Distribute a parental support survey to determine employees' wants and needs.

    C. Research parental support programs that are being used by other companies.

    D. Develop plans for an onsite childcare facility that is available to employees.

7. A global HR business partner (HRBP) is asked to design a performance management process. Which process should the HRBP suggest for managing a globally diverse workforce?

    A. A pay-for-performance-based appraisal system

    B. Performance evaluations based on peer feedback

    C. An entitlement approach to employee evaluation

    D. A forced distribution performance appraisal process

8. How can an organization implementing a 401(k) retirement program reduce its compliance burden by increasing its adherence to the Pension Protection Act of 2006's regulations?

   A. Offer a cash balance pension plan.

   B. Sponsor plans that facilitate automatic enrollment with default contributions.

   C. Propose an employee stock ownership plan.

   D. Offer a deferred profit-sharing plan.

9. A small HR department that uses a reliable HRIS platform is ready to invest in an applicant tracking system (ATS). Which step should the HR manager take before deciding to purchase a new ATS?

   A. Speak to vendors about upgrading the current HRIS platform with cutting-edge technology.

   B. Inform employees that HR will be investing in an ATS.

   C. Meet with vendors to discuss integrating the ATS into the current HRIS platform.

   D. Draft a project plan to transition from manual applicant tracking to the new ATS.

10. Which outcome best measures the successful transfer of knowledge from a training program?

    A. Satisfaction with training content

    B. Job performance improvement

    C. Cross-training ability

    D. Behavior modeling

11. After several employee incidents, an organization conducts a risk assessment and identifies substance use as a priority for HR to address. Which best represents HR's responsibility to support a substance-free workplace?

    A. Require employees suspected of substance usage to seek counseling through the employee assistance program.

    B. Ensure the organization is sharing the clearly outlined substance use policy's expectations with all employees.

    C. Contract with a local provider to accommodate onsite substance use testing for employees directly after incidents occur.

    D. Train managers to document suspected employee substance use behavior in the event an employee must be terminated.

12. Which factor is most crucial for maintaining a leadership pipeline?

    A. Executive coaching

    B. Succession planning

    C. Performance counseling

    D. Emotional intelligence development

13. Why might a manufacturing company with just-in-time production prefer Lean Six Sigma over a traditional total quality management approach?

A.   Lean Six Sigma concentrates on quality that conforms to internal requirements.

B.   Lean Six Sigma focuses on improving efficiency by decreasing the amount of waste.

C.   Lean Six Sigma encourages rapid responses from all aspects of the business to quality changes.

D.   Lean Six Sigma reworks the critical path of task dependencies based on the quality of each constraint in the process.

14. An HR executive requests an opportunity to develop their skills in managing people. The HR director plans to select and assign a coach to the executive. Which is the most important criterion in the selection of a coach?

A.   Tenure in a role similar to the one held by the executive

B.   Project management certification

C.   Positive results in a recent 360-degree feedback exercise

D.   High-performance appraisal ratings

15. Which best describes an effective employee volunteering program?

A.   A cosmetic surgery company sends volunteer doctors to other countries on a cleft palate repair mission.

B.   An advertising company recruits diver volunteers for coral propagation in a highly-populated coastal area.

C.   A financial services company sponsors volunteers for relief goods distribution to recent typhoon victims.

D.   A medical research company grants employees paid leave to volunteer if they refer a participant for clinical trials.

16. Senior leadership asks HR to implement a benefits package to attract and retain key talent in the company. Which would be the most effective benefit to include?

A.   Sign-on bonus

B.   Health savings account

C.   Assigned parking spot

D.   Flexible work schedule

Section 2: This section has eighteen situational judgment items (SJIs).

The following scenario goes with the next two items.

An employee in a midsize organization reports to both an internal manager, who is in the same department as the employee, and an external manager, who is in another department. In a recent performance review, the internal manager rated the employee as not meeting expectations while the external manager indicated that the employee's performance was satisfactory. The external manager also noted that the employee has not been receiving sufficient support from the internal manager, and indicated that the employee had various extenuating circumstances, including family member deaths and personal illness, which influenced key deadlines and deliverables. The employee filed a grievance about the poor performance review from the internal manager, claiming that their performance was sufficient and the internal manager never indicated a performance problem during the year. The HR director is asked to address the grievance.

17. Compensation decisions for individual employees are based partly on performance ratings. How should the HR director determine the employee's overall performance rating for the year?

    A.   Compute the overall performance rating by averaging the two managers' ratings.

    B.   Host a meeting with the managers to resolve differences in their performance ratings.

    C.   Facilitate a meeting with the managers and the employee to discuss what the rating should be.

    D.   Obtain additional performance reviews from the employee's colleagues.

18. Organizational policy does not provide guidance on how to conduct performance reviews for employees whose performance is impacted by illness or other personal challenges. Which solution should the HR director recommend to organizational leaders?

    A.   Request that the employee's manager and HR review each employee's situation on a case-by-case basis when an employee is impacted by illness or personal challenges.

    B.   Require that managers base their ratings on performance that occurs during the period of the year when an employee is not affected by personal challenges.

    C.   Direct managers to rate performance during periods of personal challenge separately then create a mathematical formula to combine that rating with the regular performance rating.

    D.   Exclude legally protected leave from the performance review process but ask managers to include other types of leave when making ratings.

The following scenario goes with the next two items.

An entry-level assistant at a private research institution is departing the institution to begin a new job. A highly published and well-known senior researcher at the institution sends an email to the assistant regarding the upcoming departure. In the email, the senior researcher criticizes the assistant's work and calls the assistant various derogatory names. The senior researcher mistakenly copies the email to the entire research program of 30 people. A midlevel program administrator forwards the email to the HR director stating that the senior researcher frequently makes verbally abusive comments to entry-level staff members. The HR director responds by dismissing the senior researcher's actions. The program administrator then emails the issue to the chief human resource officer (CHRO).

19. The program administrator explains to the CHRO that some staff members are afraid to report the senior researcher to the HR director. Which is the first action the CHRO should take to encourage staff to report inappropriate behavior?

    A.   Review the institution's policy to ensure it includes protections for staff members who report inappropriate behavior.

    B.   Install a lockable box on the premises to collect employees' anonymous comments.

    C.   Speak with the HR director to discuss appropriate responses to employee complaints.

    D.   Meet with individual staff members privately to discuss their concerns regarding the HR director.

20. The institution's chief operating officer makes a public statement claiming the allegations of the senior researcher are false. Which action should the CHRO take to ensure the entire leadership team understands how this statement impacts organizational performance?

    A.   State to the leadership team that HR cannot achieve its mission if senior leaders' decisions overrule institutional policy.

    B.   Present case studies to the leadership team that convey the consequences of tolerating inappropriate behavior at work.

    C.   Present to the leadership team a policy revision that forbids public communication on sensitive topics until they are resolved internally.

    D.   Explain to senior leadership how the public announcement can negatively affect employee engagement and performance.

The following scenario goes with the next three items.

A non-unionized company provides construction services to several clients who have union representation. These clients require that all onsite projects be completed by union-represented craft workers. To meet this requirement, the construction services company contracts with two third-party employers to secure union-represented craft workers for the onsite project work. During the course of the work, one of the third-party employers goes out of business. Subsequently, the other third-party employer increases its price for leasing its craft workers to the construction services company.

The CEO is concerned that the construction services company will be unable to make a profit if they accept the third-party employer's new pricing but acknowledges a decision must be made soon if they are to continue to provide services to clients. The construction services company tries to pass along the increased labor cost to clients by attempting to renegotiate a few of the contracts at a higher price. However, this results in losing business from these clients. Because the HR manager has experience with negotiating labor agreements, the CEO asks the HR manager to investigate other solutions.

21. After the loss of business, an employee leaves the HR manager a voicemail stating there are rumors about layoffs and asks if the rumors are true. Since the HR manager is not certain of the company's future plans, how should the HR manager respond?

    A. Send an email to all employees stating that the company has no intentions of laying off employees at this time.

    B. Call the employee back stating that there are no plans for layoffs at this time, but the employee will be notified if those plans change.

    C. Return the employee's phone call to say that a response cannot be provided because there is a lot of uncertainty with the business right now.

    D. Plan to call the employee back once the company's future plans are definite.

22. Because of the uncertainty surrounding the business, the HR manager notices that morale is low. Which action should the HR manager take to increase morale most effectively?

    A. Host a companywide meeting to have the CEO provide an update on the state of the company.

    B. Encourage workgroups to have daily team huddles at the beginning of each workday.

    C. Provide financial rewards to employees who are performing well despite the uncertainty surrounding the business.

    D. Distribute training funds to all managers so they can promote the professional development of their direct reports.

23. The HR manager learns that some of the company's former clients hire a main competitor. This competitor is trying to lure talented employees away from the company. Which action should the HR manager take to ensure the company retains its employees?

    A.   Increase the salaries of all employees so that their pay exceeds the market rate for their positions.

    B.   Hire external talent whom other employees will want to collaborate with on projects.

    C.   Offer growth opportunities to employees to help them understand themselves and their career objectives.

    D.   Establish a culture that focuses on high performance and results.

The following scenario goes with the next two items.

A multinational resort hotel chain's executive officers decide to implement a quality improvement program across all properties in two years to help the chain win a highly coveted international award. The program focuses on improving guest experiences, improving monthly quality metrics, and increasing profitability. To impress the executive officers, the general manager of a large resort property hires a new HR director to oversee and complete the implementation of the program in six months.

However, the resort employees have not dealt effectively with large change management efforts in the past due to poor communication and planning. The resort's senior managers frequently exhibit interpersonal conflict during all-employee meetings. In addition, employees are given very little time and funding to attend training, and the general manager frequently prioritizes guests' needs before the needs of staff and facilities.

24. The HR director discovers that the resort does not have a process for collecting HR metrics, and senior managers have a limited understanding of data analytics. How should the HR director promote the usefulness of data for business decisions?

    A. Deliver a senior manager briefing demonstrating how HR metrics represent organizational performance.

    B. Deliver a senior manager briefing describing basic processes for collecting and analyzing HR data.

    C. Meet with senior managers individually to discuss the processes they use to make HR and business decisions.

    D. Implement an all-employee engagement and retention survey to demonstrate the benefits of collecting HR metrics.

25. The HR director determines that HR needs to implement an employee development and succession planning initiative to meet the requirements of the quality improvement program. Which action should the HR director take to build consensus among the senior managers to support the initiative?

    A. Prepare a draft implementation plan outlining the process and requirements of the initiative for the senior managers to review.

    B. Prepare a senior manager briefing that highlights how the initiative will build credibility for the resort and the entire hotel chain.

    C. Present a business case to the senior managers describing how employee performance and guest experience will improve.

    D. Advise the senior managers to consider the negative consequences of failing to meet the requirements of the quality improvement program.

The following scenario goes with the next two items.

In a manufacturing company, two factory employees submit a complaint to HR claiming that working in the factory has worsened underlying non-life-threatening medical conditions. They worked in the factory as machine operators for three months and worked in a similar industry for over 15 years. Both employees report frequent reactions and had to leave work on multiple occasions. The factory has a high safety rating from independent safety monitoring groups, but the employees present a news article to HR that the factory's main product is a substance that has affected them negatively.

The employees submit a transfer request to the HR manager to work in the sales department where there is less exposure to the main product. However, their skill sets do not match those required for sales employees. The HR manager is also concerned that other employees may perceive the transfer as unfair because the pay is higher in the sales department than in the factory.

26. After hearing that the two employees requested a transfer from HR, other factory employees began to make similar requests. How should the HR manager manage employees' expectations about transfer requests?

    A. Notify all employees they should contact HR for any work-related problems or dissatisfaction with the job before submitting a transfer request.

    B. State that employee transfer requests will be carefully reviewed by hiring managers for alignment with company needs.

    C. Update company policy to establish a limit on the number of employees who can apply for a transfer at any given time.

    D. Establish a cross-training program for the factory employees to learn skills in other departments.

27. Other employees express concerns that the company's main product causes similar health-related issues and believe the factory is an unsafe place to work. Which action should the HR manager take to address the employees' concerns?

    A. Consult with HR managers at industry competitors on whether employees need better personal protective equipment.

    B. Conduct monthly training for all factory employees about practicing necessary safety protocols.

    C. Lead a focus group of factory managers to see if they have any safety concerns about the factory.

    D. Request a separate independent safety monitoring group to review the company's main product for safety concerns.

The following scenario goes with the next three items.

In a large retail organization, a store director is accused of discriminatory behavior toward a department manager of a different ethnicity than the store director. The department manager sends a letter to the corporate headquarters stating that the way the store director treats the department manager creates a hostile work environment and makes the department manager uncomfortable. In the letter, the department manager claims that the store director's behavior stems from the department manager's ethnicity. The HR director at the store, who reports to the corporate HR department and the store director, is contacted by corporate HR to investigate the situation. The HR director contacts the store director and the department manager to notify them of the investigation.

28. Word of the investigation soon spreads among store employees, and a division begins to arise between those who support the department manager and those who support the store director. How should the HR director restore unity within the store?

   A. Organize a storewide mentorship program pairing individuals of differing opinions.

   B. Hire an external organization to conduct diversity training for all employees.

   C. Create a multicultural engagement team to identify opportunities to build employee unity.

   D. Conduct an all-employee meeting to review corporate expectations and policies regarding workplace harassment.

29. Although the investigation is supposed to be confidential, by the time the investigation is complete and a verdict is reached, rumors surrounding the investigation are circulating throughout the organization. How should the HR director address the rumors?

   A. Acknowledge that an investigation of the store director has been ongoing but provide no details.

   B. Provide department managers with basic details to share within their teams.

   C. Hold a meeting with all employees to address the rumors and answer questions.

   D. Supply managers with a list of expectations and talking points about any rumor discussions they observe.

30. The investigation reveals that the department manager's perception of hostile treatment stems from cultural differences because the way the store director leads is different from the department manager's experience with leadership. How should the HR director address the cultural differences?

   A. Provide cultural sensitivity training for all leaders working at the store.

   B. Assign cultural sensitivity training for all employees working at the store.

   C. Speak with organizational leaders to identify opportunities to discuss different cultures.

   D. Establish an ongoing diversity initiative to promote cultural awareness among employees.

The following scenario goes with the next two items.

A small IT product company grew from 50 employees to 250 employees in eight years and has been able to sustain an organizational culture that values employee loyalty and strong interpersonal relationships. Most of the company's project leaders have been with the company since its founding. The company's annual organizational climate survey consistently indicates that employees enjoy working with each other. Recently, the company agreed to a merger with a larger, multinational firm. The multinational firm's HR director is tasked with determining how job roles and responsibilities will change as the companies merge.

The merger causes employees to feel anxious about job security, resulting in a slowdown in productivity. As part of this process, the HR director determines that one of the IT company's project leaders needs to shift to a new position in a new department. All positions in the project leader's current department have been filled with the multinational firm's senior software engineers. The HR director offers the project leader several different positions but the project leader refuses each one. The project leader is well-known and has a large span of influence among other company staff.

31. The project leader decides to resign. Given the project leader's large span of influence, which is the best way for HR to communicate the resignation to the employees from the original, small IT company?

    A. Ask the project leader to notify direct reports of the departure.

    B. Notify all employees of the project leader's departure via email.

    C. Inform direct reports of the project leader's departure via email.

    D. Organize meetings with direct reports to notify them of the project leader's departure.

32. Employees throughout the company are expressing frustration that their current job roles and responsibilities will change. Which approach by the HR director would be most effective to ensure that employees are satisfied with their new roles in the merged company?

    A. Provide employees with training to obtain additional skills for their new roles.

    B. Offer bonuses to reassigned employees, with larger bonuses for more difficult reassignments.

    C. Train managers to recognize employee engagement issues then conduct interventions when necessary.

    D. Conduct an online employee satisfaction survey to provide extra resources to teams with the lowest satisfaction.

The following scenario goes with the next two items.

During a routine inspection of a manufacturing plant work area, the HR director notices a piece of cardboard on the floor behind a machine. The HR director tells the operations supervisor the cardboard should be removed because it is a safety hazard. The operations supervisor says employees use the cardboard while engaging in religious practices and removing it will upset them. The operations supervisor informs the HR director that because the company does not provide a private space for employees to engage in religious practices, as a result, employees create their own space. The operations supervisor insists that all employees need a private space to attend to personal matters, such as taking personal phone calls or administering medications because employees currently resort to using the bathrooms or their personal vehicles to find privacy. The HR director promises to act immediately to find a solution.

33. The HR director meets with the HR team members to discuss the issue and learns that none are aware of the employees' engagement in religious practices at work. Which action should the HR director take?

    A. Recommend the HR team members express their appreciation to the operations supervisor for supporting employees' expression of religious values.

    B. Advise the HR team members to speak with the operations supervisor to learn more about employees' religious practices.

    C. Direct the HR team members to replace the piece of cardboard with safer alternatives.

    D. Suggest the HR team members conduct research to understand the employee's religious practices.

34. The HR director meets with the leadership team to advocate for providing a dedicated space for all employees to safely attend to religious matters. The operations VP opposes this by saying the plant should not adapt to individual practices. How should the HR director respond to the opposition?

    A. Meet with the operations VP privately to explain why the VP's comment is not appropriate.

    B. Ask the operations VP to identify which religious practices the plant should accommodate.

    C. Advise the operations VP that the prevalence of religious practices might change over time.

    D. Notify the leadership team that HR will collaborate with operations to request quotes for building a dedicated space in the plant.

Section 3: This section has sixteen knowledge items (KIs).

35. An organization's ethics report shows a steady increase in ethical violations. The most commonly cited reason for violations is a lack of knowledge of the company's code of ethics. Which action should management take to reduce the number of violations?

A.   Identify the first-time offenders to have them undergo ethics training.

B.   Send a companywide email to remind employees of the code of ethics.

C.   Hold employee group meetings to discuss the report then address ethics-related concerns.

D.   Inform all employees that they should direct ethics-related questions to HR.

36. Which scenario presents the lowest security risk when implementing a new HRIS?

A.   Essential team members leaving the organization before the new HRIS is fully operational

B.   Privacy breach of employee confidential information

C.   Ineffective employee training and change management communication

D.   Unrestricted access to employees' dummy data during HRIS's pilot stage

37. Which type of organization expects and rewards risk-taking to develop skills?

A.   Mechanistic

B.   Participative

C.   Learning

D.   Authoritarian

38. A company plans to open several branches in an area heavily populated by residents who do not speak the company's operating language. Which initiative displays the alignment of the HR workforce strategy with the company's strategic direction?

A.   Create a telephone service that can serve clients in multiple languages.

B.   Analyze languages spoken by current employees to proactively recruit to fill any gaps.

C.   Develop an online tool that finds the nearest location where staff speak the customer's language.

D.   Pursue a strategic partnership with local area businesses to staff the new branches with foreign nationals.

39. Which belief characterizes ethnocentrism?

    A. Every culture is equally valid so others have no right to impose their culture's values on another's culture.

    B. Differences between one's own and other cultures are insignificant.

    C. One's personal needs and welfare are more important than those of others.

    D. New cultures should be judged according to the standards of one's own culture.

40. Which process enables an HR professional to determine the positions that require additional personal protective equipment in a health facility?

    A. Job audit

    B. Job analysis

    C. Job design

    D. Job specification

41. Which is an advantage of outsourcing HR functions?

    A. Provides access to specialized expertise.

    B. Increases internal service levels.

    C. Assists with the identification of new HRIS technology.

    D. Guarantees legal compliance for global mobility.

42. An HR director is facilitating an organizational redesign effort in preparation for a new product launch. Which is a benefit of using a matrix model for the redesign?

    A. Accelerates the organization's response to market changes.

    B. Creates collaboration between different departments.

    C. Minimizes overhead costs for the product launch.

    D. Pushes decision-making to lower levels of the organization.

43. A quality control manager wants to identify problems in work processes and then use rigorous measurement to reduce variation and eliminate rework. Which technique will help the quality control manager train employees to provide quality products?

    A. Six Sigma

    B. Lean Enterprise

    C. Total Quality Management

    D. Theory of Constraints

44. Which is the shared goal of providing both performance feedback and coaching to an employee?

   A.   Identifying below-average performance

   B.   Providing career support

   C.   Improving interpersonal skills

   D.   Developing skills for better performance

45. How is the show your work technique of knowledge management best applied in an organization?

   A.   Require subject-matter experts to complete a manual of standard operating procedures.

   B.   Create an internal shared drive then encourage all employees to store their files on it.

   C.   Build an internal organizational platform for proactive knowledge sharing with employees.

   D.   Establish standard templates for employees to use to freely ask for needed information.

46. An organization's performance management program is revamped to address a lack of performance, productivity, and engagement. Which is the most important element for the HR manager to maximize the effectiveness of the program?

   A.   The program is regularly evaluated and improved.

   B.   The program is benchmarked against other programs within the industry.

   C.   A task force is formed to provide input on the program.

   D.   A consultant who specializes in the areas included in the program is hired.

47. An HR director needs to develop a risk assessment to determine the potential of losing high-performing employees. Which best describes a risk assessment that uses a quantitative technique?

   A.   Probabilistic

   B.   Residual

   C.   Tolerance

   D.   Diversifying

48. Despite a competitive benefits package, a consulting firm's HR director consistently receives feedback indicating associates are displeased with the total rewards package. The executive team decides to re-evaluate the total rewards approach to improve effectiveness, but no additional budget is allotted. Which action should the HR director take first?

A. Conduct an employee satisfaction survey on the total rewards package to repurpose the budget around the highest-scoring areas.

B. Determine what the organization wants to achieve to see if rewards are aligned with this target.

C. Benchmark the current benefits and compensation offerings against external market data.

D. Research total rewards packages offered by competitors then implement best practices.

49. An ongoing conflict between two employees results in them refusing to work together or trying to find a solution to their problem. Which form of alternative dispute resolution should HR deploy in this case?

A. Dialectic method

B. Conciliation

C. Conflict triangle

D. Facilitation

50. Which is the best demonstration of HR consultation in an organization's hiring processes?

A. Posting the job openings on a variety of online forums

B. Translating complex employment laws into actionable items

C. Attending career fairs at local colleges and universities

D. Ensuring the applicant tracking system remains updated

Appendix 1

The SHRM-SCP Practice Test Answers

Question Number	Item Data		Rationale
1	**Domain**	**Business**	"Provide measurable, value-adding deliverables that impact company key performance indicators" is correct because HR managers can validate initiatives by providing deliverables that will positively impact key performance indicators (KPIs). An example of this would be connecting improved sales employee retention rates to the achievement of sales goals.
	Sub-Competency	**Business Acumen**	
	Difficulty	**Somewhat Easy**	
	Key	**A**	
2	**Domain**	**Workplace**	"Train managers on what constitutes a protected concerted activity" is correct because participation in investigation proceedings is a protected activity. Retaliation actions include non-promotion and it is unlawful to retaliate against an employee engaged in protected activities under Equal Employment Opportunity statutes.
	Sub-Competency	**US Employment Law & Regulations**	
	Difficulty	**Somewhat Hard**	
	Key	**C**	
3	**Domain**	**People**	"Evaluate pay based on competitors" is correct because organizations need to know and understand what the market pay is for their jobs and job families, which allows the organization to set pay levels and determine pay for each job. Without the salary survey data, a company may create inequities, overpay, underpay, and increase turnover due to unsatisfactory pay ranges.
	Sub-Competency	**Total Rewards**	
	Difficulty	**Somewhat Easy**	
	Key	**C**	
4	**Domain**	**Workplace**	"Offshoring" is the correct answer because offshoring includes running a portion of the company's business in another location and, depending on the location, labor in that location may be less expensive than the company's home country.
	Sub-Competency	**Managing A Global Workforce**	
	Difficulty	**Somewhat Easy**	
	Key	**B**	
5	**Domain**	**Organization**	"Facilitate conversations about individual preferences on ground rules for the team's members" is correct because when team members openly discuss their preferences and expectations up front, the team stands a better chance of functioning well and achieving objectives.
	Sub-Competency	**Organizational Effectiveness & Development**	
	Difficulty	**Hard**	
	Key	**C**	

6	Domain	People	"Distribute a parental support survey to determine employees' wants and needs" is correct because employees may want or need various types of support or benefits from the program and the HR manager needs to better understand the employees' needs before looking for a solution.
	Sub-Competency	Employee Engagement & Retention	
	Difficulty	Somewhat Easy	
	Key	B	
7	Domain	Interpersonal	"A pay-for-performance-based appraisal system" is correct because attributes of performance-driven evaluation processes that emphasize contributions and outcomes can be customized, such as individual versus team incentives, to fit the cultural dimensions of the globally diverse workforce while still creating an equitable program of rewarding employees.
	Sub-Competency	Global Mindset	
	Difficulty	Somewhat Easy	
	Key	A	
8	Domain	Workplace	"Sponsor plans that facilitate automatic enrollment with default contributions" is correct because the Pension Protection Act of 2006 requires employers to auto-enroll their employees in a 401(k) plan that is offered by the employer. The employer must provide a stated percentage of the employee's compensation at the time of auto-enrollment.
	Sub-Competency	US Employment Law & Regulations	
	Difficulty	Easy	
	Key	B	
9	Domain	Organization	"Meet with vendors to discuss integrating the ATS into the current HRIS platform" is correct because ensuring that the new system will integrate with the existing system will increase the effectiveness of the ATS, making the company's investment yield better output. Without a system of record to provide strong integrations between these solutions, it can be a disjointed and ineffective experience.
	Sub-Competency	Technology Management	
	Difficulty	Somewhat Easy	
	Key	C	
10	Domain	People	"Job performance improvement" is correct because training transfer is the extent to which skills and knowledge learned in training are applied on the job, which can be measured by evaluating changes in job performance.
	Sub-Competency	Learning & Development	
	Difficulty	Easy	
	Key	B	
11	Domain	Workplace	"Ensure the organization is sharing the clearly outlined substance use policy's expectations with all employees" is correct because HR's responsibility includes developing preventive employment policies and procedures that reduce the organization's exposure to risk across the entire employee population, regardless of employment location or type.
	Sub-Competency	Risk Management	
	Difficulty	Easy	
	Key	B	

12	Domain	Organization	"Succession planning" is correct because it is a proactive workforce planning process that centers around internal employee career development to attain the skills needed for key organizational roles.
	Sub-Competency	Workforce Management	
	Difficulty	Easy	
	Key	B	
13	Domain	People	"Lean Six Sigma focuses on efficiency by decreasing the amount of waste" is correct because Lean Six Sigma in manufacturing environments with just-in-time production can reduce the quantity of waste which impacts resources and alleviates production issues since supply does not come from excess stock.
	Sub-Competency	Hr Strategy	
	Difficulty	Hard	
	Key	B	
14	Domain	Leadership	"Positive results in a recent 360-degree feedback exercise" is correct because people management skills are best taught by some-one who has good management practices and positive experiences to share with the coachee or trainee. The 360-degree feed-back exercise measures and evaluates the people-related skills of a people manager.
	Sub-Competency	Leadership & Navigation	
	Difficulty	Somewhat Hard	
	Key	C	
15	Domain	Workplace	"A cosmetic surgery company sends vol-unteer doctors to other countries on a cleft palate repair mission" is correct because sending volunteers to other locations best describes an effective employee volunteer-ing since the company leveraged its core knowledge components and turned it into a charitable cause.
	Sub-Competency	Corporate Social Responsibility	
	Difficulty	Hard	
	Key	A	
16	Domain	People	"Flexible work schedule" is correct because a flexible work schedule allows employees to have a better work–life balance, which is something that impacts employees at all levels.
	Sub-Competency	Total Rewards	
	Difficulty	Easy	
	Key	D	
17	Domain	Interpersonal	
	Sub-Competency	Relationship Management	
	Difficulty	Somewhat Easy	
	Key	B	
18	Domain	Business	
	Sub-Competency	Consultation	
	Difficulty	Somewhat Hard	
	Key	A	

19	Domain	Interpersonal
	Sub-Competency	Communication
	Difficulty	Somewhat Hard
	Key	A
20	Domain	Interpersonal
	Sub-Competency	Communication
	Difficulty	Somewhat Easy
	Key	D
21	Domain	Interpersonal
	Sub-Competency	Communication
	Difficulty	Easy
	Key	B
22	Domain	Leadership
	Sub-Competency	Leadership & Navigation
	Difficulty	Somewhat Easy
	Key	A
23	Domain	Business
	Sub-Competency	Business Acumen
	Difficulty	Easy
	Key	C
24	Domain	Business
	Sub-Competency	Analytical Aptitude
	Difficulty	Somewhat Easy
	Key	A
25	Domain	Leadership
	Sub-Competency	Leadership & Navigation
	Difficulty	Somewhat Easy
	Key	C
26	Domain	Interpersonal
	Sub-Competency	Communication
	Difficulty	Somewhat Easy
	Key	B

Situational judgment items (SJIs) require the examinee to think about what is occurring in the scenario and decide which response option identifies the most effective course of action. Other response options may be something you *could* do to respond in the situation, but SJIs require thinking and acting based on the best of the available options. Do not base your answer on your organization's approach to handling the situation; rather, answer based on what you know *should* be done according to best practice. Panels of SHRM-certified subject matter experts rate the effectiveness of each response option, and the *best* answer is derived by statistical analysis of those expert opinions.

27	Domain	Business
	Sub-Competency	Analytical Aptitude
	Difficulty	Easy
	Key	D
28	Domain	Leadership
	Sub-Competency	Inclusion & Diversity
	Difficulty	Somewhat Easy
	Key	C
29	Domain	Interpersonal
	Sub-Competency	Communication
	Difficulty	Somewhat Hard
	Key	D
30	Domain	Leadership
	Sub-Competency	Inclusion & Diversity
	Difficulty	Easy
	Key	D
31	Domain	Interpersonal
	Sub-Competency	Communication
	Difficulty	Easy
	Key	D
32	Domain	Business
	Sub-Competency	Consultation
	Difficulty	Hard
	Key	C
33	Domain	Leadership
	Sub-Competency	Inclusion & Diversity
	Difficulty	Hard
	Key	D
34	Domain	Leadership
	Sub-Competency	Leadership & Navigation
	Difficulty	Easy
	Key	A

Situational judgment items (SJIs) require the examinee to think about what is occurring in the scenario and decide which response option identifies the most effective course of action. Other response options may be something you *could* do to respond in the situation, but SJIs require thinking and acting based on the best of the available options. Do not base your answer on your organization's approach to handling the situation; rather, answer based on what you know *should* be done according to best practice. Panels of SHRM-certified subject matter experts rate the effectiveness of each response option, and the *best* answer is derived by statistical analysis of those expert opinions.

35	Domain	Organization	"Hold employee group meetings to discuss the report then address ethics-related concerns" is correct because employee group meetings will provide a venue to immediately address questions where management can proactively clarify uncertainties about the existing code of ethics.
	Sub-Competency	Employee & Labor Relations	
	Difficulty	Somewhat Easy	
	Key	C	
36	Domain	Workplace	"Unrestricted access to employees' dummy data during HRIS's pilot stage" is correct because when an HRIS is being tested or in a sandbox environment for demonstration, employees' personal data should be safeguarded. Using dummy data will protect employees' data when more users have access to the system during implementation, making it the lowest security risk.
	Sub-Competency	Risk Management	
	Difficulty	Somewhat Hard	
	Key	D	
37	Domain	People	"Learning" is correct because the focus is on rewarding skill development at the expense of risk-taking.
	Sub-Competency	Employee Engagement & Retention	
	Difficulty	Somewhat Easy	
	Key	C	
38	Domain	Organization	"Analyze languages spoken by current employees to proactively recruit to fill any gaps" is correct because recruitment is an activity that HR is responsible for when aligning with a company's strategic direction.
	Sub-Competency	Structure Of The HR Function	
	Difficulty	Somewhat Hard	
	Key	B	
39	Domain	Leadership	"New cultures should be judged according to the standards of one's own culture" is correct because ethnocentricism is the belief that one's home conditions are best, which interferes with understanding the behavior of other cultures.
	Sub-Competency	Inclusion & Diversity	
	Difficulty	Hard	
	Sub-Competency	D	
40	Domain	People	"Job analysis" is correct because job analyses assess all aspects of the job from the requirements, and conditions, to the knowledge, skills, abilities, and other attributes, and context the jobs are performed.
	Sub-Competency	Talent Acquisition	
	Difficulty	Somewhat Hard	
	Key	B	
41	Domain	Organization	"Provides access to specialized expertise" is correct because HR-specific functions can be outsourced to specific services with an increased level of expertise not previously possessed by internal staff that can benefit the company.
	Sub-Competency	Structure Of The HR Function	
	Difficulty	Somewhat Easy	
	Key	A	

42	**Domain**	**Organization**	"Creates collaboration between different departments" is correct because a matrix model creates functional and divisional partnerships that focus on the work. The matrix model creates a better overview of the market for employees working on products other than what is within the strict confines of their department or functional area.
	Sub-Competency	**Organizational Effectiveness & Development**	
	Difficulty	**Somewhat Easy**	
	Key	**B**	
43	**Domain**	**People**	"Six Sigma" is correct because Six Sigma is a methodology that helps improve business practices by identifying an issue and correcting it so that it does not appear again, resulting in improved quality.
	Sub-Competency	**Hr Strategy**	
	Difficulty	**Somewhat Hard**	
	Key	**A**	
44	**Domain**	**Interpersonal**	"Developing skills for better performance" is correct because both processes aim to improve performance through deliberate, guided communication.
	Sub-Competency	**Communication**	
	Difficulty	**Easy**	
	Key	**D**	
45	**Domain**	**Organization**	"Build an internal organizational platform for proactive knowledge sharing with employees" is correct because in the show your work technique of knowledge management employees proactively share their work to ensure continuity and retention of knowledge and not merely save their work. As such, it is critical to have a secure, internal platform where employees can freely share their work. There is a focus on how they do their work and their experience in doing their work, and not just what work they do.
	Sub-Competency	**Workforce Management**	
	Difficulty	**Somewhat Easy**	
	Key	**C**	
46	**Domain**	**People**	"The program is regularly evaluated and improved" is correct because performance management programs that are refined to address organizational needs cannot stay stagnant and expect the same level of results in the ever-changing business environment. To achieve maximum effectiveness the program must undergo routine evaluation to determine how to continually best serve the organization's needs.
	Sub-Competency	**Employee Engagement & Retention**	
	Difficulty	**Somewhat Easy**	
	Key	**A**	
47	**Domain**	**Workplace**	"Probabilistic" is correct because probabilistic is a quantitative technique that estimates the likelihood of situations that have not yet occurred.
	Sub-Competency	**Risk Management**	
	Difficulty	**Somewhat Easy**	
	Key	**A**	

48	Domain	People	"Determine what the organization wants to achieve to see if rewards are aligned with this target" is correct because HR must first confirm what the organization wants to achieve to determine how the total rewards package can help in the achievement of its strategic goals before measuring or evaluating rewards. The alignment of the program with strategic goals will then allow HR to customize the package within reason.
	Sub-Competency	Total Rewards	
	Difficulty	Hard	
	Key	B	
49	Domain	Organization	"Conciliation" is correct because a neutral third party acts as a communication conduit between disputing parties. This is appropriate when conflicting parties need to reach a mutually agreeable decision or solution.
	Sub-Competency	Employee & Labor Relations	
	Difficulty	Hard	
	Key	B	
50	Domain	Business	"Translating complex employment laws into actionable items" is correct because specific, comprehensive HR expertise that is not easily acquired by other members of the organization is translated into a tangible action for the organization's improvement and/or success. This action will also help safeguard the organization from legal risk.
	Sub-Competency	Consultation	
	Difficulty	Somewhat Easy	
	Key	B	

Appendix 2

Twelve-Week Study Schedule Template

We have provided a set of study schedule templates to guide your SHRM-SCP exam preparation. Please use these spaces to create your plan and write it down.

Planned Test Date with Prometric: _____

Study Week 1: _____

Weekly Goal: This week, I will...

_____

_____

_____

_____

	Planned Time	Study Focus
Sunday		
Monday		
Tuesday		
Wednesday		
Thursday		
Friday		
Saturday		

Study Week 2: _____

Weekly Goal: This week, I will...

_____

_____

_____

_____

	Planned Time	Study Focus
Sunday		
Monday		
Tuesday		
Wednesday		
Thursday		
Friday		
Saturday		

Study Week 3: _____

Weekly Goal: This week, I will...

_____

_____

_____

_____

	Planned Time	Study Focus
Sunday		
Monday		
Tuesday		
Wednesday		
Thursday		
Friday		
Saturday		

Study Week 4: _____

Weekly Goal: This week, I will...

_____

_____

_____

_____

	Planned Time	Study Focus
Sunday		
Monday		
Tuesday		
Wednesday		
Thursday		
Friday		
Saturday		

Study Week 5: _____

Weekly Goal: This week, I will...

_____

_____

_____

_____

	Planned Time	Study Focus
Sunday		
Monday		
Tuesday		
Wednesday		
Thursday		
Friday		
Saturday		

Study Week 6: _____

Weekly Goal: This week, I will...

_____

_____

_____

_____

	Planned Time	Study Focus
Sunday		
Monday		
Tuesday		
Wednesday		
Thursday		
Friday		
Saturday		

Study Week 7: _____

Weekly Goal: This week, I will...

_____

_____

_____

_____

	Planned Time	Study Focus
Sunday		
Monday		
Tuesday		
Wednesday		
Thursday		
Friday		
Saturday		

Study Week 8: _____

Weekly Goal: This week, I will…

_____

_____

_____

_____

	Planned Time	Study Focus
Sunday		
Monday		
Tuesday		
Wednesday		
Thursday		
Friday		
Saturday		

Study Week 9: _____

Weekly Goal: This week, I will...

_____

_____

_____

_____

	Planned Time	Study Focus
Sunday		
Monday		
Tuesday		
Wednesday		
Thursday		
Friday		
Saturday		

Study Week 10: _____

Weekly Goal: This week, I will...

_____

_____

_____

_____

	Planned Time	Study Focus
Sunday		
Monday		
Tuesday		
Wednesday		
Thursday		
Friday		
Saturday		

Study Week 11: _____

Weekly Goal: This week, I will...

_____

_____

_____

_____

	Planned Time	Study Focus
Sunday		
Monday		
Tuesday		
Wednesday		
Thursday		
Friday		
Saturday		

Study Week 12: _____

Weekly Goal: This week, I will…

_____

_____

_____

_____

	Planned Time	Study Focus
Sunday		
Monday		
Tuesday		
Wednesday		
Thursday		
Friday		
Saturday		

About SHRM Books

SHRM Books develops and publishes insights, ideas, strategies, and solutions on the topics that matter most to human resource professionals, people managers, and students.

The strength of our program lies in the expertise and thought leadership of our authors to educate, empower, elevate, and inspire readers around the world.

Each year, SHRM Books publishes new titles covering contemporary human resource management issues, as well as general workplace topics. With more than one hundred titles available in print, digital, and audio formats, SHRM's books can be purchased through SHRMStore.org and a variety of book retailers.

Learn more at SHRMBooks.org.

Index

A

Ace Your SHRM Certification Exam ix, 1, 43
Application process for SHRM certification exams x
    early-bird application deadline x
    transfer fees and x
Applications accepted starting date x
Assessment 39
Authorization-to-test (ATT) letter x

B

BASK. *See* SHRM BASK
Behavioral competencies 4, 18–23
    clusters of 6–7
    exam item distribution and 35
    knowledge, skills, abilities and other
        characteristics (KSAOs) and 4
Business 6, 35

C

Conflict management 19
Conflict resolution strategies 18–21
Corporate social responsibility (CSR) knowledge
    area 7
Critical evaluation 8

D

Distribution of items 1–2

E

Early-bird application deadline x
Elements of the HR function 14
Eligibility for SHRM-CP and SHRM-SCP exams xi
Exam blueprint for the SHRM Senior Certified
    Professional (SHRM-SCP) exam 35–42
Exam fee x
Exam items
    distribution by content and exam type 35
    foundational knowledge items (FKIs) 1–2
    knowledge items (KIs) 1–2
    most effective response and 44
    quantity of 1–2
    situational judgment items (SJIs) 1–2
    types of 1–2
    unscored 2
Exam structure 1–2
    distribution of items by content and exam type 35
Exam study plan 36–40. *See also* Self-assessment
    creating a SMART study plan 40–41
    self-assessment for 36–40
    SHRM BASK and 40
    study blocks 40
    study schedules 41
    twelve-week study schedule template 69–82

Exam timing 2
    early-bird application deadline and x

F

Foundational knowledge items (FKIs) 1–2

H

HR expertise 4
    domains of 6
    example 13–17
HR knowledge domains 35
    exam item distribution and 35
HR technical competency 4
    HR expertise and 4

I

Interpersonal 6, 18, 35
Interpreting self-assessment 39. *See also* Self-assessment
Item types 8–9
    knowledge items (KIs) 8
    situational judgment items (SJIs) 8–9

K

Key concepts (KCs) 7
    how to study 9
    steps to identifying 10
Knowledge 4
Knowledge items (KIs) 1–2, 8, 25–27, 32–34, 44–47,
    57–60
    critical evaluation 8
    problem-solving 8
    recall 8
    understanding 8
Knowledge, skills, abilities and other characteristics
    (KSAOs) 4

L

Leadership 6, 35

O

Operational-level HR duties 3
Organization 6, 13, 35

P

People 6, 35
Practice items ix. *See also* SHRM-SCP practice test
Problem-solving 8
Proficiency indicators (PIs) 3, 7
    how to study 9
    parallel 7
    SHRM-SCP vs. SHRM-CP 7
    steps to understanding 11
Prometric testing centers x

R

Recall 8
Relationship management 18–23
    key concept 18–19, 18–20
    proficiency indicators 19–23
Remote-proctored testing xii

S

Scheduling. *See also* Study schedules
    early-bird application deadline x
    study template for 69–82
Self-assessment 36–40. *See also* Exam study plan
    instructions for 36
    interpreting 39–40
    scoring 39
SHRM
    member benefits x
    website 1
SHRM BASK ix, 3. *See also* Behavioral competencies;
    HR expertise
    blueprint for the SHRM-CP and SHRM-SCP
        exams 3
    creating a study guide from 9–11
    exam study plan and 40
    how to study using 8–11
    HR technical competency and 4
    individuals testing outside of the U.S. and 3, 24
    key concepts (KCs) 7
    SHRM Senior Certified Professional (SHRM-SCP)
        exam and 3
    structural difference in 7
    structure of 4, 5
SHRM Body of Applied Skills and Knowledge.
    See SHRM BASK
SHRM Certified Professional (SHRM-CP) exam,
    eligibility for xi
SHRM Learning System ix, 44
SHRM-SCP practice test 43–60
    vs. certification exam 43–44
SHRM Senior Certified Professional (SHRM-SCP)
    exam ix
    application process x
    candidates for ix
    distribution of items 1–2
    early-bird application deadline x
    eligibility for xi
    exam blueprint 35–42

exam structure 1–2
exam timing 2
fee for x
how to apply x
individuals testing outside of the U.S. and 3, 24
item types 8
practice items ix
practice test 43–60
practice test answers 61–68
practice tests vs. 43
proficiency indicators for 3
remote-proctored testing and xii
SHRM BASK and 3
SHRM Certified Professional (SHRM-CP) vs. ix
SHRM study guide. *See Ace Your SHRM
    Certification Exam*
strategic-level HR knowledge and ix
types of items 1
SHRM study guide. See *Ace Your SHRM Certification
    Exam*
Situational judgment items (SJIs) 1–2, 8–9, 28–31,
    48–56
    major components of 8
Skills 4
SMART study plans 40–41
Standard application deadline x
Strategic-level HR functions and responsibilities 3
Strategic-level HR knowledge ix
Structure of the HR function 13–17
    key concepts 13–15
    proficiency indicator 15–17
Study blocks 40
Study plans. *See* Exam study plan
Study schedules 41
    twelve-week template 69–82

T

Testing centers, Prometric x
Timing of exam 2
Transfer fees x
Types of exam items 1

U

Understanding 8
Unscored exam items 2

W

Workplace 6, 35

Maximize your chances for success on the SHRM-SCP® exam.

HR professionals who prepare for SHRM certification with the SHRM Learning System® consistently beat the average exam pass rate. Moreover, candidates who prepare using both the SHRM BASK® and the SHRM Learning System are 42% more likely to pass the SHRM-SCP exam.

The interactive SHRM Learning System provides a customized roadmap to guide you throughout your studies.

1 **Customized Study Plan**: As you progress through the system, your personal study plan dynamically adapts to your activity and serves up the most crucial content for you to study.

2 **Online Learning:** Fill your knowledge and competency gaps with interactive online reading content (with optional audio segments) that teaches the entire SHRM BASK. Assess your understanding with flashcards and quizzes.

3 **Practice Questions:** Test your knowledge and increase exam day confidence with 2,700+ practice questions presented through online quizzes and a practice exam that includes questions previously used on actual SHRM Certification exams.

4 **Topic Cards:** Visualize your study plan through a series of course topic cards depicting SHRM BASK topics. Click on a card to access a topic and study activities. As you complete a topic, another will take its place in your study plan.

5 **Bonus Resources:** The SHRM Learning System includes a digital copy of the *Ace Your SHRM Certification Exam study guide*, which includes study guidance, test-taking tips as well as additional practice questions.

Give yourself the best chance to succeed on the SHRM-SCP exam with the SHRM Learning System. To learn more, visit **https://www.shrm.org/credentials/certification/exam -preparation.**